Educational Implications of Qur'an

About the Authors

Dr. Samina, Associate Professor and Head, Department of Education (Integrated course—B.A., B.Ed. and B.Sc., B.Ed.), Maulana Azad University, Jodhpur, Rajasthan, India served since 2007 as Lecturer in Geeta Bajaj Women Teachers Training College, Jaipur, University of Rajasthan and since 2009 as Lecturer in Maulana Azad Muslim Teachers Training College, Jai Narain Vyas University, Jodhpur and since 2017 as Associate Professor and Head, Department of Education, Maulana Azad University, Jodhpur, Rajasthan, India. She taught Pedagogy of English, Pedagogy of Urdu and Educational Psychology at undergraduate level. Her field of research specialisation is Educational Psychology of the Holy Qur'an. She attended various workshops and she has presented a number of papers in National Seminars.

Dr. Anjali Sharma, Associate Professor and Head, School of Education,Central University of Rajasthan, India served since 1998, as Assistant Professor in Teacher Education at College for Teacher Education (CTE), University of Rajasthan and since 2014 as Associate professor and Head, Department of Education at Tezpur Central University, Assam in North East Region, India. She taught Pedagogy of Science and Educational Administration, Planning and Financing, Evaluation and Assessment and Research Methodology. She has published around more than fifty research paper and articles in peer reviewed and refereed journals at national and International level and did some research project to evaluate about educational policies and programmes offered by State Government of Rajasthan, India. She organized a number of programmes throughout her career, i.e. Workshops and Seminar and contributed at various levels as research supervisors, examiner, resource person, experts and member of various committees.

Educational Implications of Qur'an

Samina
Anjali Sharma

CONCEPT PUBLISHING COMPANY PVT. LTD.
NEW DELHI-110059

ISBN-13: 978-93-86682-57-4

First Published in 2019

Published and Printed by

Since 1974

Concept Publishing Company Pvt. Ltd.
A/15-16, Commercial Block, Mohan Garden,
New Delhi-110059 (INDIA)
T : 91 11 25351460, 91 11 25351794
E : publishing@conceptpub.com; *W* : www.conceptpub.com

Cataloging in Publication Data--Courtesy: D.K. Agencies (P) Ltd. <docinfo@dkagencies.com>

Samina (*Associate professor of education*), **author.**
Educational implications of Qur'an / Samina, Anjali Sharma.
pages cm
Includes bibliographical references and index.
ISBN 9789386682574

1. Education--Religious aspects--Islam. 2. Qur'an--Criticism, interpretation, etc. I. Sharma, Anjali (Associate professor of education), author. II. Title.

LCC BP134.E38S26 2019 DDC 297.122837 23

DEDICATED

TO

OUR PARENTS

Preface

The problem before any individual is how to live in the world and live completely and successfully. And it is mainly the job of education to resolve that problem and put the child on the right track. The education of today is devoid of its basic merits. The current educational system, whether given a local tinge or made up in a foreign fashion, is quite incompatible with our ideals and sentiments. The modern education is predominantly rationalistic. It has become mostly naturalistic or biological and therefore, does not pay due regard to the moral, the religious and the spiritual aspect of man. An ideal education is that which along with the physical and the intellectual aspects aims at developing the spiritual aspect of man. It is this concept of ideal education which is contained in the teachings of the Holy Qur'an and Hadith.

In this research work the plan followed, for the exposition of the values and principles of the Qur'an and its Educational implications is like this: First chapter discusses about the brief introduction of Islam, five pillars of Islam, Islamic concept of Education, related literature and justification of the problem. Islam is not merely a religion or faith; it is a way of life, a complete code of conduct. It guides its followers on the path of a successful life. Five pillars of Islam are Faith, Prayer, Fasting, Charity and Pilgrimage. Faith in Allah and His Prophets, action in accordance with that faith, and the realization of one's relation to God as a result of action and obedience. To keep away from evil, wickedness and to purify from bad deeds are realities of the prayer. Fasting is a stepping stone to Righteousness. Physically he does not eat, drink or smoke or have sexual intercourse. Spiritually, he abstains from all evil thoughts, actions and sayings. Charity is a means of purification. It is given at a fixed proportion of 2.5 per cent of one's annual savings to the needy persons. Its foremost purpose is to sow the seeds of kindness, sympathy and benevolence. *Hajj* is a compulsory pilgrimage to weaken the love for the world. This also symbolizes the unity and the oneness of Mankind.

Objectives of Islamic Education or Qur'anic Education are—To obtain knowledge of reality, Transfer of knowledge and experiences from generation to generation, Purification of mind and rearing of high moral values, Harmonious development of body mind and soul, Character building is the ultimate aim of Qur'anic Education. Researcher wants to depict importance of Qur'an and Hadith for students, teachers and society. How can the guidance of Qur'an and preaching of Prophet Mohammad can be beneficial for the students, teachers and our society, this is the objective of the present research.

Second Chapter consists of the Content of the Qur'an. **The Qur'an is the pure word of God**. Not one word therein is not divine. Not a single word has been deleted from its text. The Book has been handed down to our age in its complete and original form since the time of Prophet Muhammad. The Holy Qur'an claims to be Book of Hidyah, i.e. Guidance, for man. It is a Book that is available to all mankind –indeed it addresses itself, by and large, to the totality of mankind. Its message is relevant to different peoples living in different parts of the world. Further, its message is valid for all times to come – in other words, it is not a Book that will ever be out of date. Some permanent values, some selected human rights and standards of a good character which are taken from the Qur'an have been mentioned. They are taken in their original Arabic form, from the Holy Qur'an, with their English Translation. They are bearing responsibilities, fulfilment of promises, justice, virtuousness, charity, knowledge, understanding, patience, tolerance, purity, proper use of wealth etc. Some rights and duties are – high regard for mankind, gender equality, justice for everyone, safeguard chastity, no boundation of religion, freedom of spouse, fulfilment of promises etc. Some everyday manners which have been discussed are – manners of meeting each other, manners of conversation, manners of greeting each other, manners of eating and drinking, vain talks and deeds should be avoided, backbiting strictly prohibited, physical and mental cleanliness, due regard to parents etc.

In the third chapter a critical analysis has been done according to the objectives and an attempt has been made to find out how the values of the Holy Qur'an could be helpful for the teachers, students and the society. First objective of the study is – to analyse the duties and characteristics of the teacher mentioned according to the Message of Qur'an. The success of education depends as much on the skillful teaching of the subjects as on the fitness of the curriculum. Much depends on the teacher himself. It is the personality of the teacher, his efficiency and superior human qualities that influence the intellectual and the spiritual growth of the child. A teacher is not a man of mean status: he is a maker of men. He builds up children to fit in the general social frame and guides their destinies to their final goal. An ideal teacher is necessarily a man of firm and unshakable faith, he is a man of very strong character, courage and confidence and therefore, unstopping to intimidation and immoral pulls of the outside forces. A teacher should consider Prophet Mohammad SAW as his role model and should go through the values and duties which are given in the Qur'an.

Second objective of the study is – to study guidance and preaching of the Qur'an which could be helpful for the students. The learner should pay high regard to his teacher. Al Ghazali says the learner is a patient and the educator is his physician. Silence has been lavishly praised in Hadith. It is related that one who keeps silence gets salvation. It is said that the learned are the physicians of the society and that wealth is the ailment of the society. The learners are expected to maintain external neatness as well as internal purity. A learner or a child should be obedient and should respect his parents. It is next to worship of Allah. Spying and backbiting are like eating one's brother's flesh according to Qur'an. Learners should remain away from such ill habits.

Third objective of the study is – To study the role of Qur'an and Preaching of Prophet for the benefit of the society. Progress of a society depends considerably on its teachers and students. The nation's well-being depends on teacher's well-being. No society can afford to neglect him. The teacher, above all, is the social engineer and social worker. He is the maker of the history; he is the maker of the society. The Qur'an has enforced an etiquette which has definitely a far reaching influence in establishing cordial relations and brotherhood. It is laid down in the Qur'an that children in a family, whether young or grown up, should not be allowed to be slipshod and vulgar in their talk, dress and manners, lest they should get into bad habits eventually. Selfless service to mankind irrespective of the considerations of caste, creed or kinship is the most glorifying deed of a true human being.

Fourth Objective of the study is – to study the Educational Implications of Qur'an. The Qur'an is the unique book. It is the fountainhead of all knowledge and wisdom, the source of divine inspiration, the best and most reliable code of human code of human conduct and the only guide to truth and salvation. It must be made the basis of all education and be made compulsory at all levels according to the requirements of age and comprehension, because it teaches discipline and obedience, and by virtue of its human character gets sanctified and the correct sense of value is developed.

Fourth chapter includes a brief of Philosophy of the Holy Qur'an. In this chapter metaphysics, epistemology and axiology according to the Qur'an and their educational implications have been discussed. Philosophy is considered as a guide to the good life of man because knowledge about the nature of things. The Qur'ānic universals provide us with the surest and most perfect guidance in all matters like actions, manners, morals, values, patterns of behaviour of the people; in fact all the ways of life. They suit all times and all peoples. According to Qur'an; there is only One Supreme Lord of the Universe. He is Omnipotent, Omnipresent and the Sustainer of the world and of mankind. It is an important metaphysical concept and answers the riddles of the universe. Islam gives a revolutionary concept of the unity of mankind. The Prophet came to unite humanity on the word of God and make the dead live again.

The attitude of the Qur'an to knowledge and its acquisition is very positive and emphatic. Time and again it declares that acquisition of knowledge from any source and at any cost is the ordained duty of the believer. Qur'an assigns third place – only next to God and His angels – to those who possess knowledge, and rightly so. The Qur'an approaches human problems realistically and in a serious and dignified manner. It offers the very best of practical and final solutions to them. These solutions are final because no better solution is possible for human intellect to think of.

Fifth chapter consists of conclusion, limitations, and suggestions. Man is not isolated in the accomplishment of his task of life. He has been made to live in a large society, with the assistance and cooperation of which he becomes able to maintain and develop his individual personality. In the world he has been assigned a specific part to play; his satisfactory performance depends upon the skillfulness, efficiency and integrity with which he seeks the support of his society and plays that part. He has some social responsibilities which he has to perform. Progress of a society depends considerably on its teachers and students. Selfless service to mankind irrespective of the considerations of caste, creed or kinship is the most glorifying deed of a true human being. Charity or *Zakat* has been made compulsory on the eligible 'scheduled' (*sahibe Nisab*) persons. It awakens a sense of social responsibility in man, organizes human beings in a society and a state and enjoins the individual to subscribe to the social good. It also inculcates feelings of sympathy and love for the mankind in general and for the poor and afflicted in particular. A man's strength lies in his unity with his kinsfolk, friends and fellow men.

Qur'an's guidance and Prophet's preaching are like a vast Ocean. It covers whole Universe, whole humanity, and complete way of life. So, study has been limited to only educational implications of Qur'an and students, teachers and society are taken into consideration. Present work is confined only to a brief study of Educational Implications of Qur'an and Hadith and it contains only those chapters of my Dissertation which are directly related to education. Only some permanent values of the Holy Qur'an some selected Human Rights and Obligations and standards of a good character according to the Holy Qur'an have been chosen and tried to find out their educational implications. All the values and all rights of Qur'an could not be enumerated and explained here. Therefore, this study is confined to explain only those universals which have a direct bearing on the educational philosophy. Educational philosophy of the Holy Qur'an in brief.

In this dissertation an effort has been made to analyse the values and principles of the Holy Qur'an which should be adopted by the teachers and the students for brightening their character and for the reformation of the society. As we know that growth the development of the child depends on the teaching staff and progress of the society depends considerably on the type of teachers working in it. Teachers are the backbone of our society. There is need of really good teachers who have some unique qualities about them. He is an important figure and is expected to act as social reformer, moralist, national integrator etc. A teacher should go through the Holy Qur'an and teach its values and principles to the students also. A Teacher, according to Qur'an, is a committed person. Teaching for him should not be merely a profession of life. He is committed to produce a virtuous generation of students and also assumes the responsibility of advancing the society. The teacher influences every aspect of the student's life. He is a role model for them. So, first of all he himself should translate into action the teachings that he theoretically imparts to his students. Let the world then adhere to the teachings of the Qur'an which are unquestionably genuine and beneficial, when all other instruction has failed in making the human race really literate and providing peace and happiness to the world.

Just as a growing plant needs pruning of its superfluous and irregular growth so that it may grow in proper shape and improve its flowering and fruit bearing quality, an individual child also needs constant care, check and proper training of his faculties so that he can be prevented from developing ugly traits and be helped to acquire the best human qualities which they can get under the shade of the Holy Qur'an.

Samina

Acknowledgements

"It takes hours to read a book but months to write one".

First praise is to God, the Almighty, on whom we depend for sustenance and guidance. Second, our sincere appreciation goes to that moment when we decided to work on this topic. It was very tough for both of us to me as a supervisor and my co-author as a researcher. We were not very clear that time; due to grace of God somehow we started to work on this.

We would like to express our gratitude to **Prof. Rajni Sharma,** Former Principal, Shree Agrasen Postgraduate College of Education, Jamdoli, Jaipur for providing constant support and guidance whenever needed. The nature of this work was philosophical, she was only source to us to clear our quarries related to the philosophical research method and design. We want to thank her for taking benefit of her expertise and her patient to take out time for academic help at every level.

Next, we owe a deep debt of gratitude to **Er. Gulam Nabi.** He played a major role in coming out this work. He is a good scholar of Arabian language; he helped us to translate the exact meaning of the *Aayats* of Holy Qur'an and checked the Arabian text in the manuscript. Here we want to tell that he is the father of my co-author, Samina, in this way he played another most prominent role to encourage and strengthen and to overcome obstacles. In her words, "he was always there with me at every step of my work".

We are very much thankful to Mr. Manas Dey, Executive Area

Manager, North East Region of India, Concept Publishing Co. (P) Ltd., New Delhi, who was the first person who showed keen interest in the work and guided us to proceed further. He took the lantern and showed us the path.

We would like to thank Mr. Ashok K. Mittal of Concept Publishing Co. (P) Ltd., who agreed and took initiative to bring out this research work as book. We remembered that he asked first to send two chapters and reviewed text. Finally, he valued our research work and became ready to publish that.

We are extremely thankful to Samina's mother, Rashida for her untiring service and kind cooperation, due to which it became possible to her to complete this work. She is also thankful to her every family member especially her husband Dr. Sabir Hussain and Kids Sahil and Sahrish because being wife and mother really it was very hard task to her to spare time and put whole hearted efforts but they not only cooperated her and made the time easy for her.

I also take an opportunity to express my deep sense of gratitude towards all the writers and publishers of the books and researchers, which were a great help and support to us during our tough academic time.

I wish to give special thanks to my scholar and co-author Dr. Samina whose consistent efforts and dedication towards work is the primary cause to make this book a reality. When we started the work on this topic to be honest I was really puzzled, but then her patience and hardworking nature helped me to gain confidence. I went through a lot of new things which I learnt from her and she helped me to make this book an awesome presentations.

I acknowledge with gratitude the efforts of Concept Publishing Co. (P) Ltd., New Delhi in bringing out this book.

Anjali Sharma
Associate Professor & Head
School of Education
Central University of Rajasthan
Bandarsindri, Kishangarh
Ajmer-305817

Contents

بسم الله الرحمن الرحيم

"Praise be to God, the
Lord of the worlds!
The compassionate,
The merciful!
King of the day of
Judgement !
They only do we
Worship, and to Thee
Do we cry for help.
Guide Thou us on
The Straight path,
The path of those to
Whom Thou hast
Been gracious –
With whom Thou art
Not angry, and who
Go not astray.

بسم الله الرحمن الرحيم

1
Introduction

Today, Muslims may be found throughout the world, particularly in the Middle East, North Africa, South Asia, Central Asia, and Southeast Asia. The majority of Muslims are not Arabs; only 20 per cent of Muslims originate from Arab countries. Islam is the second largest religion in the United Kingdom, and many other European countries, including France, which has the largest Muslim population in Western Europe. If current trends, continue it will soon become the second-largest religion in the United States.

Islam is the last and final religion to all mankind and to all generations irrespective of colour, race, nationality, ethnic background, language or social position. The religion of Islam is not be confused with Mohammedanism. The latter is misnomer to Islam. Muslims do not accept this name as it gives wrong information about Islam and Muslims. In the simplest term, Islam means submission to the Almighty God. Islam is a monotheistic religion based upon the Qur'an, which adherents believe was sent by God (Arabic: Allāh) through Muhammad. Followers of Islam, known as Muslims, believe Muhammad to have been God's final prophet. As a result, most of them see the actions and teachings of Muhammad as related in the *Sunnah* and *Hadith* to be indispensable tools for interpreting the Qur'an.

The word **Islam** derives from the Arabic triconsonantal root ***sīn-lām-mīm***, which carries the basic meaning of ***safety*** and ***peace***. The word islām is the noun form of aslam, a verb derived from that root, which means to accept, surrender, or submit; thus, Islam effectively means submission to God (Arabic: Allāh) and accepting him. The legislative meaning is to submit to God by singling him out in all acts of worship, to yield obediently to him and to disassociate oneself from polytheism.

'***ISLAM***' is an Arabic word. It means the act of resignation to God. The root word is *SLM*, pronounced '*salm*' which means peace form which comes the word 'aslama' which means he submitted, he resigned himself. Al-Islam or Islam is the religion which brings peace to mankind when man commits himself to God and submits himself to His will. According to the Holy Book revealed to Muhammad (peace and blessings of God be on him), this is the only true religion professed by all Prophets from Adam to Muhammad, the Last Prophet. A 'Muslim' is one who resigns himself to God and thereby professes the faith of al-Islam. A Muslim therefore believes in all the Prophets and makes no distinction between one and the other. He also believes that God has sent His prophets to all corners of the earth to preach the same religion, that His message stopped coming after the last revelations received by the last Prophet Muhammad (SAW), and that the message received by the last Prophet is the most comprehensive and the final form of God's message to Man.

> *"Those who believe and whose hearts find rest in the remembrance of Allāh – indeed it is in the thought of Allāh alone that the heart of man really finds rest – those who believe and act righteously, joy is for them, and a blissful home to return to." **(al-Qur'an, 13:28-29)***

This message was preached by all the prophets of God, who guided man to the right path. But man not only veered away from the right path again and again, but also lost or distorted the code of guidance which the prophets had bequeathed. That was why other prophets were sent to re-state the original message and guide man to the right path.

Islam defies definition but its most fundamental characteristics may certainly be delineated. But the meaning of

Islam as posited by **Sir Mohd.Iqbal** is most exhaustive. To understand that central meaning one has to appreciate a unique combination of scientific approach and validity of mystic experience. Islam embraces all knowledge, whether on the relations of man with the invisible and transcendent forces, or on the relations of man with man.

According to the **Qur'an**,

> *"...We detail our revelations for a people who have knowledge." **(9:11)**,*

> *"...Thus, we display the revelations for people who have sense" **(30:28)** and*

> *"... Thus, do we expound the revelations for people who reflect" **(10:24)**.*

Therefore, according to Islam, religion is that which is in agreement with science, reason, and reflection, and that only men of science, reason and reflection are capable of understanding religion of Islam.

Islam is not merely a religion or faith; **it is a way of life, a complete code of conduct**. It fixes the parameters of all that is in life and the world – one's routine, one's character, one's dealings, one's conduct, one's career, one's social life and above all the life hereafter. It teaches how to behave, how to earn, how to spend and how to live gracefully, It guides its followers on the path of a successful life. It also imposes sanctions and binds the believers to be fully responsible towards people around, family and friends in particular and the whole society at large. Islam, as a complete religion provides a code of conduct and a way of life for its followers. It integrates man with God, awakens in him a new moral consciousness and invites him to deal with all the problems of life – individual and social, economic and political, national and international – in accord with his commitment to God. Islam does not divide life into domains of the spiritual and the secular. It spiritualizes the entire existence of man and produces a social movement to reconstruct human life in the light of principles revealed by God. Prayer and worship in Islam are means to prepare man to fulfil this mission. Islam aims at changing life and producing a new man and a new society, both committed to God and to the welfare of mankind.

"Rabbana atena fidduniya........azabannar."

That is why **Islam** is not a religion in the limited sense of the word; rather it is a **complete code of life and a culture producing factor**. Muslim culture profits from all available sources, local and international, but its unique characteristic is that it grows from the foundations of the Qur'an and *Sunnah*.

1.1 Fundamental Principles of Islam

Faith, Action and Realization

In order to be a true 'Muslim' three things are necessary: Faith, Action and Realization:

Faith in Allāh and His Prophets, action in accordance with that faith, and the realization of one's relation to God as a result of action and obedience. The **Prophet Muhammad (SAW)** as described in a ***Hadith*** **by Bukhari** enumerated five basic principles:

Islam is built on five (things), the bearing of witness that there is no god but Allāh and that Muhammad (SAW) is the Messenger of Allāh and the keeping up of prayer and the payment of *zakat* and the pilgrimage and the *Ramadhan*. ***Faith*** which is described in the **Qur'an**, the Holy Book of Islam, as ***Iman*** consists in believing that Allāh alone is worthy of worship and that Muhammad (SAW) is the Messenger of Allāh, and is bearing witness to the above statement which is represented in the *kalmia.*

La ilaha illallahu Muhammad ur-Rasullallah.

(There is no god except Allāh and Muhammad is His Prophet).

Action, described in Arabic word '***amal***' is the manifestation in actuality how far we are true servants of God. As action needs rules and regulations according to which we organize our individual and social behaviour, the revelations and the actual physical embodiment of these revelations in the action of the Prophet provide both the basis ands structure of the Law of human conduct, know as **Sharriah**.

1.2 Five Pillars of Islam

Besides ***Iman*** **(*faith*)** which provides the central pillar that sustains the whole structure, the four other pillars in the four corners are: ***Prayer (salat), Fasting (sawn), Charity (zakat), Pilgrimage (Hajj).***

Salat (prayer): A Muslim has to pray five times a day, before sunrise, between mid-day and afternoon, in the afternoon, immediately after sunset and between the time when the twilight is over and just before dawn. It means he cannot be forgetful of his dependence of Allāh and derives sustenance and new initiatives and strength this remembrance. Prayer prevents from evil. *Salat* (prayer) is a compulsory form of worship, which is like an exercise towards which man is attracted with interest and willingness. He offers it continually, so that his life may be free from all diseases and the body may be healthy and strong. The holy Qur'an and the *Sunnah* of the Prophet both are the open proofs of these realities. To keep away from evil, wickedness and to purify from bad deeds are also realities of the prayer. When Allāh commanded the compulsory prayers to be established, He **stated** its wisdom in this way:

*"**Prayer prohibits obscenity and erg.**"*

Fasting is a stepping stone to Righteousness: Similarly, Islam has made fasting compulsory. He fasts for one lunar month in a year, every day from dawn till sunset, the month of *Ramadhan.* Physically, he does not eat, drink or smoke or have sexual intercourse. Spiritually, he abstains from all evil thoughts, actions and sayings. In other words he tries to realize his true self by striving to realize within himself some aspects of the divine character. The Prophet (SAW) has said:

> *"Fasting is not the name of merely keeping away from eating and drinking, but it is keeping away from wicked and obscene things. If in the state of fasting, someone abuses you or picks up a quarrel with you, say: "I am fasting."*

Zakat is a means of purification: Charity (*Zakat*) implies that everything that he seems to possess belongs to Allāh and therefore anyone in need has a share in it and he should willingly and gladly help individuals and society when they are in need. *Zakat* has been made compulsory on the eligible **'scheduled'** (*sahibe Nisab*) persons. It is given at a fixed proportion of **2.5 per cent of one's annual savings** to the needy persons. It is not merely a tax that is collected from the pockets of the people, but its foremost purpose is to sow the seeds of kindness, sympathy and benevolence, and to provide a change of introduction among the various sections of the society and to establish the relationship of love and friendliness. The purpose of paying *Zakat* has been stated in the **Qur'an** in the following words:

"O Prophet! Take charity from their property so that it may clean them and purify them" (Tauba: 103)

***Hajj* is a compulsory pilgrimage to weaken the love for the world:** Pilgrimage to Makka, i.e. *Hajj* implies Man's temporary suspension of all worldly activities and his realization of himself as a naked soul in front of Allāh alone. This also symbolizes the **unity** of the Muslim Ummah and the **oneness of Mankind**. Giving commands about this compulsory worship, Allāh states:

> *"The months of Hajj are well-known. In these months whoever intends to perform Hajj should not indulge in sexual act, wicked act, and fighting during the Hajj. Whatever righteous act you will perform will be known to Allāh". (Baqarah: 197)*

All these four are intimately tied up with all other aspects of man's individual and social behaviour. By following them and thereby living a life of complete dedication to the Will of Allāh, a man becomes a true Muslim. Therefore *salat*, *sawn*, *zakat*, *Hajj* and other forms of worship like these are the stepping stones for real perfection, and are the means of cleanliness and purity that make life secure and magnificent. On account of high attributes and noble qualities that are the inalienable parts and the consequences of these forms of worship, they have been given a very high and important place in Allāh's religion.

A Muslim is one whose outlook on life is permeated with this consciousness. He is committed to the values of life given by the Qur'an and the *Sunnah.* He tries to live according to the guidance given by God and His Prophet and he strives to promote the message of Islam through his word and actions. This striving is known as **Jihad** which means a striving and a struggle in the path of God. *Jihad* has been described in the Qur'an and the *Sunnah* as the natural corollary of these pillars of faith. Commitment to God involves commitment to sacrifice one's time energy and wealth to promote the right cause. It may be necessary at times to give one's life in order to preserve Truth. *Jihad implies readiness to give whatever one has, including life, for the sake of* Allāh.

Islamic philosophy tells us that every human being has been sent to this earth with a certain aim. The God almighty has bestowed upon the mankind all sorts of gifts and kindness. However, with these comes a sense of responsibility and dutifulness which one has to abide by.

1.3 Islamic Concept of Education

The concept of education in Islam must not only provide for the herein but also for the hereafter. It should provide knowledge not only for the mind but also for the soul. It should be based not only on perception but also intuition. It should give more emphasis on learning and bringing up and less on instruction and teaching. Muslims have long-range view of life, which spreads over the two worldly lives. The Muslim education should prepare the individual for all the stages of the two lives. It is possible if proper guidance given to the individual at each stage. The individual should maintain his individuality based on Islamic principles and change the polluted environment to it rather than changing himself according to the environment.

Muslims have not only long-range view of life but also a broader and higher view of life. The Muslim education should not only make allowance for the development of body, mind and soul on Islamic lives but should also throw light on whole being of the individual to give purpose to his life. Islam believes in one and only one God. The Islamic concept of education should also do the same. It should be the aim of Muslim as an individual as well as of Muslim society. The Muslims should develop as much qualities of God in themselves as much as possible. They should try to identify themselves with the life of the Prophet Mohammad. This relationship with God and His messenger should not only be verbal but also be reflected in their action.

Islam not only provides guidance for living life but also clearly tells about dangers which may astray an individual or society from the right path. **Bilgrami** writes,

> *"The concept of knowledge in Islam is to provide for all the securities in this life and also in the life to come. There may be a sense of security for the present life attached to the concept of learning in the Western way of thinking, but the knowledge that provides for the security here and also in the hereafter is completely missing in the Western concept of education. It is only the education based on Islamic principles that provides for a complete sense of security at all stages of this long vision of life and, therefore, better equips and individual for dealing with the problems of his daily life with wisdom, with firmness and with absolute morality."*

1.4 Objectives of Islamic Education or Qur'anic Education

1.4.1. To Obtain Knowledge of Reality

Durrani discussing the objectives of Muslim education says—

"The objective of education is to obtain knowledge of reality and captivation of natural phenomena, but life should not be unbridled wisdom and thought".

Allama Iqbal, explaining the meaning of theory of education in Islam mentions—

"The fostering of self, training, wakefulness, construction and stability in fundamental principles".

1.4.2.Transfer of Knowledge and Experiences from Generation to Generation

In Islam the concept of education depend upon its past. The events mentioned in the Qur'an and occurred during the time of Prophet Mohammad are like torch-bearing minaret. Collective feelings, experiences and traditions have basic share in the growth and development. Therefore, reading of history and learning lesson from it is basic necessity of education. Islam is purely educational movement. It has no restrictions on learning of modern sciences and neither the modern sciences are against Islam.

Ahmed says:

"The overall objective of education should be to transfer to the new generation the accumulated knowledge's, insights and experiences of past generation and to guide it at once to extend and expand this heritage and to develop that individual character which is enlightened and pure and disciplined enough to enable them to prefer the collective good to personal gain and live as part of a society of universal human brotherhood."

1.4.3.Purification of Mind and Rearing of High Moral Values

Hashmi is of the opinion that objective of Muslim education is to prepare human beings who obey God and ready to do any thing for His pleasure and possess high Islamic and moral values. ***Zaman*** discussing Muslim education writes—

"The objective of education is purification of mind and make people cultured and courteous. Thus with education rearing up is also necessary which rearing up of mind and intellect on the one hand and rearing of character, action and of body."

She is of the opinion that children should develop the habits of truth, honesty and hard work so they do not commit any theft or dishonesty inside and outside the school. They should develop the sacrifice as second nature and such qualities, which make tolerance, respect for elders, love for younger and favour and grace to peers as a part of their character.

1.4.4. Harmonious Development of Body Mind and Soul

Hasan writes in his paper "Islamic System of Education"—

"It is to provide for the most harmonious development of body, mind and soul in a way that an individual is not only able to achieve what is best in the present life, but what is most beneficial for his soul when it leaves the body. The concept of learning must provide security not only here, but also in the hereafter. In self-expression it will not merely lay emphasis on knowledge for the mind, but will also include the knowledge for the mind, but will also include the knowledge that is essential for the soul. It will not rest content merely with perception but will also call for intuition – a higher form of intellect; it is more concerned with attitude and understanding than with mere teaching. It exhales people for their motives, but also Judges them by their actions." It may be concluded that the objective of education in Islam is the creation of the "**good and righteous man**" who worships God in the true sense of the term, builds up the structure of his earthly life according to the Muslim Jurisprudence and employs it to sub serve his faith.

1.4.5. Character Building is the Ultimate Aim of Quranic Education

There is a saying coming down from ages that if wealth is lost, nothing is lost; if health is lost, something is lost; but if character is lost, everything is lost. Character gets strength only when we are confronted with a situation which we have to choose between higher and lower values and we voluntarily sacrifice the lower value of "**immediate gain**" for a more solid and higher value of seeking the "**Face of Allāh**". Choosing the higher value is an act of "**Faith**" – yes, faith which carries forth every object of the Universe, step-by-step, to its self-fulfillment and self realization.

1.5 Education and the Qur'an

The very first verse which was revealed to the Prophet Mohammad (saw) was as follows:

> *"Read in the name of thy lord who creaqteth; He creaqteth man from a clot. Read: And thy lord is the Most Bounteous, Who teacheth by the pen, teacheth man that which we knew not".* ***(Surah Al-Alaq 1-5)***

There are two important points for consideration in this revelation from God to the Prophet. Firstly, it was the first revelation and education was considered so important for Muslims that the prophet was told about reading, teaching, pen and knowledge in the very first message. Secondly, it was conveyed to that man who was himself not educated. He could neither read not write. The **Qur'an** has several verses, which highlight the importance of knowledge, education, teaching and teacher etc. Some of them are referred to here:

> *"Say (unto them, O Mohammad): Are those who know equal with those who know not? But only man of understanding will pay heed".* ***(Surah Al-Zamar – 9)***

The verse clearly makes distinction between who possess knowledge and those who do not possess. Islam thus grants high status to those who attain knowledge. Islam clearly guides Muslims to attain knowledge. Islam clearly guides Muslims to attain knowledge if they want to rise in comparison to others.

"O my Lord! Advance me in knowledge"

(Surah Al Ta-ha—114)

God is above every human event or desire. His purpose is universal. But he is the Truth, the absolute Truth; and his Kingdom is the true kingdom that can carry out its will. We should always pray for increase in our knowledge, which can never at any given moment be complete.

> *"God will exalt those who believe among you and those who have knowledge to high ranks. God is informed of what ye do."* ***(Surah Al-Mujadla—11)***

The Qur'an says that those who attain knowledge they will be exalted high ranks. These verses clearly tell that those who have been given knowledge and those who believe in God will be raised in ranks.

The **Prophet Mohammad** said:

> *"No present or gift out of all the gifts and presents to a child is superior to a good liberal education".*
>
> ***(Trimidhiy and Bayhaqiy)***

1.6 Related Literature

No Researcher starts his work in isolation. He takes the benefit of knowledge, which has been accumulated on the basis of the work done by the researchers in the past. It is difficult to fine the research studies, which are identical in nature. Thus, the researcher has to depend upon these studies, which are directly or indirectly related to the study. The review of literature indicates the clear picture of the problem to be solved. Reviewing the literature of the field can develop the scholarship in the field. A quantitative and qualitative analysis of this research usually gives the worker an indication of the direction. It is considered the most important pre-requisite to actual planning and conducting the study. For any specific research project to occupy this place in the development of a discipline, the researcher must be thoroughly familiar with both previous theory and research.

Researcher analyzed **Buch Surveys** and various **Educational Abstracts** published by **N.C.E.R.T.**

1.6.1. In Vol. I of Fourth Survey of Research in Education of **M.B. Buch,** Pandey conducted **A Comparative Study of Educational Philosophy in Gita and Koran** from Kumarkam University in 1985. (71)

The study was designed to make a comparative of the Educational Philosophy propounded in the *Gita* and *Qur'an*. It also aimed at highlighting the practicability of Educational Ideas of these scriptures in present day India. The researcher has tried to give a critical description of the Educational Philosophy in these two texts. He has studied translation of the originals and has tried to collect commentaries on them by philosophers, educational leaders and educationists. Some of the specialists in the area were interviewed by the researcher and while formulating the results of the study, their views were also given due weight age.

The **Main findings** of the study were: (1) According to the *Gita*, the living being is a part of *Brahma* and it aims at uniting with *Brahma* through *moksh*. (2) *Moksh* can be achieved through good deeds, i.e. *nishkam karma*. (3) According to the *Qur'an*, living beings are created by God and when a living being dies his soul has to wait till the say of Judgement and then, according to the balance of his good or bad deeds he is sent to *Jannat* or *Dozakh*. (4) According to the *Gita*, education should lead to all round development and curriculum should have a wide variety of subjects to achieve this aim. (5) In the *Gita* stress is laid on the importance of the teacher but, at the same time, it is said that the individuality of the child should not be suppressed. In the *Qur'an* also, the importance of teacher is emphasized, but stress is also laid both on the student of religion and subjects which can be of use in life.

1.6.2. In the Vol.II of Fifth **Buch Survey** (1988-92) Ansari conducted a 1988 by on **Educational Philosophy as found in Islamic Culture** from the **University of Bombay**. This is quite good work. (17)

Problem: The study examines and analyses the Islamic Concept of Knowledge and Education – its aims, types, methods and practice – and outlines the philosophy of Islamic Education.

Objectives: (1) To find out the importance given to education in the *Qur'an* and the *Hadiths*. (2) To examine the concepts, types and aims of education stressed by the Islam. (3) To study the role of the teacher and expectation from students in Islamic Culture. (4) To study the role of the family with regard to education, the methods followed, the importance given to women's education, moral education, physical education and education of exceptional children in Islamic Culture. (5) To study the concepts of discipline and intervenalism as found in Islamic culture. (6) To suggest changes in the pattern of education to resolve its problems making education relevant and effective and promoting higher education.

Methodology: Historical method. Data: from *Qur'an* and *Hadith*, Religious Scholars Interview.

Findings: (1) The aims of Islamic Education were realization of eternity, truth, perfect living and inculcation of democratic values.

(2) Is education advocated the use of inductive-deductive method, questioning, experimentation and discussion. (3) Different curricula were planned for different stages of education. (4) The teacher was the role model for students and enjoyed a high status in society. (5) The teacher student relationship was cordial. (6) Most of the schools were single teacher schools. The system was flexible and monitorial system was in prevalence. (7) Education was obligatory for males and females and was a life long process, though formal schooling started at five years of age. (8) Women's education and art education were given prominence. (9) The Islamic philosophy of

education advocates development of universal and objective values as being the ultimate. (10) Islamic education made s significant contribution in the fields of mathematics, physics, philosophy, biology, astronomy, pharmacology and agriculture. (11) Islam advocated universal brotherhood and dignity of man, equality, social justice, freedom for all, tolerance, forbearance, welfare measures for the progress of humanity and the development of human nature in its entirety. (12) Islamic education gave importance to acquisition of Knowledge. (13) Islamic education was by and large religion centered and emphasized equilibrium between spiritual and material needs.

1.6.3 In Indian Educational Abstract. January 1997, Issue 2, **Nehvi and Lidhoo** conducted study on **Educated Muslim Women in Kashmir their Attitude Towards Tradition verses Modernity**. (60)

Problem: It aims to study the attitude of Muslim women with respect to tradition *vs.* modernization.

Objectives: (a) To assess and evaluate the attitude of Muslim women towards tradition *vs.* modernization on the basis of urban and rural background. (b) To compare the attitude of Educated women to tradition *vs.* modernization on the basis of socio-economic status (high and modern); and (c) To compare the attitude of educated Muslim women towards tradition *vs.* modernization on the basis of subject streams, i.e. science *vs.* arts and social sciences.

Methodology: The sample comprised 413 female students in B.A. /B.Sc. final year from the districts of Srinagar.

Major Findings: 1. On the basis of urban and rural background it was found that the difference between two groups as regards attitude towards modernization and traditionalism were significant. 2. The high socio-economic group (Urban subjects) had shown a progressive attitude towards modernization as compared to low socio-economic status. 3. Comparing the attitude scores of high socio-economic status urban group and high socio-economic status rural group, it was found that the high socio-economic status (HSES) urban group was progressive towards modernization and change as compared to rural high socio-economic status group. 4. The difference between low socio-economic status (LSES) urban and low socio-economic status (LSES) rural had been found to be significant. 5. LSES urban group had a positive attitude towards modernization as compared to LSES rural. 6. The responses of the Science subjects were positive and in favour of modernization where as the responses of the arts and social science subjects were tradition and ritualistic. 7. The urban educated Muslim women were more progressive and desirous of major change in the traditional mode of life. 8. There was a significant difference between the attitude of educated Muslim women with LSES and urban background as against their counterparts, i.e. the educated Muslim women with LSES with rural background.

1.6.4 **Farias** has done study on **Religious Commitments of Muslim students in Bangalore: A Study of Relationship between Religion and Social Situation.** (32)

1.6.5 **Rajwade** has done his study on the topic, **Status of Muslim Women in Indore City—A Case Study**, (Ph.D. Sociology, Indore University). (80)

1.6.6 **M. Agarwal** has done study on the topic: **A Study of the Impact of Education on Social and Cultural Modernization of Hindu and Muslim Women**, from Kumarkam University in 1980. (1)

1.6.6 In Issue 4, *Journal of Psychological Researches*, **A Study of Religiosity and Values** has been done by **Sayed Firoj and Karunanidhi** in 1995. (32)

1.6.7 **Gupta** has done his study on **Equality of Educational Opportunity and Muslims**, Bhopal University in 1980. (38)

1.6.8 **Sufi *(1941)* (91) has made a thorough Study of the evolution of Curriculum in the Muslim Educational Institutions of India from the Period of Turks and Afghans to the Period of British Rule**. He finds that the curriculum during the period of Turks consisted of the Qur'an, Calligraphy, Grammar, Poetry, Traditions, Arithmetic, Algebra, Geometry, Geography, Astronomy, Islamic Law, History, Medicine and Alchemy. During the period of **Afghan** he finds that the

Curriculum consisted of Grammar, Literature, Logic, Islamic Law, Principles of Islamic Law, Qur'anic Commentary, *Hadith*, Mysticism and Scholasticism.

1.6.9 The **Shah Waliullah** gave turn to the Islamic studies in the direction of **Philosophy**. His own course of studies which covers the period of Aurangzeb consisted of Grammar, Rhetoric, Philosophy, Logic, Scholasticism, Islamic Law, Astronomy, Mathematics, Medicine, Tradition etc. (96)

1.6.10 **Shalabi** (1954) (85) has also done study on the **curriculum** and he is of the opinion that in Muslim world it has been felt from the very beginning that educational curriculum should be according to needs and call of future life. Shalabi is of the view that the beginning of education through the Qur'an is Islamic way and all Muslim Countries agree on it. The teacher always wanted to serve knowledge and literature and wanted to teach more and more instead of concentrating on one child even if he belonged to ruler's family. The mosques were important centres of Muslim education. In the first forty years of Islam they were mainly used for the purpose of teaching. He finds three types of teachers from socio-economic status – teachers of children, preceptors and teachers of mosques and Madarsas. The teachers of children did not enjoy respect. The preceptors and teachers of mosques and Madarsas enjoyed a very high status.

1.6.11 **Rizvi** (1986) (84) has also done study on **curriculum** and he finds that this curriculum has very justifiably become useless today. According to him this curriculum evolved during the course, differentiating itself gradually as the new needs arose. It has been under revision off and on during the Muslim rule. About India he finds evidence that the last revision took place in 1747 AD through the efforts of Mulla Nizamuddin Muhammad Sihaalvi.

Rizvi (1986) has done his studies on **aim of Muslim Education** and he is of the view that **ultimate aim of Muslim education is to prepare individuals who live in a society which is just and in which the idea of omnipresence and omnipotence of God as well as a belief in His Justice predominates.** Rizvi finds that Islam does not limit education to mere theoretical learning, but includes its **practical application**, which cannot be learnt except through practical demonstration by a teacher. He concludes that in Islamic educational system a teacher has to be given rights and privileges in consideration of his duties and responsibilities. Besides these, Rizvi has also written on the importance Islamic Education for the society and the teachers. Shalabi has also concentrated on the importance of Islamic education for teachers. Rizvi finds that Islamic philosophy of education is not rigid, diehard and dogmatic which may create disdain in the mind of **"modern man"**. They do not reflect Islamic philosophy of education as they violate its very basic principle, dynamism.

1.6.12 **Qureshi** (1960) (76) in his research study on **Muslim Education and Learning in Gujarat** (1297-1758) finds the similarity in the form and content of Muslim education in Gujarat and other countries. He finds it similar because they were based on Islam everywhere. He finds intellectual unity in Muslim education on account of religion in spite of so much political disintegration in the Muslim world. Besides the religion he considers Arabic language and the learning predicated on Islam also responsible for it. He finds that theology was the backbone of the curriculum of Muslim education in Gujarat as well as anywhere in India. He finds that system of education in Islam remained **"inflexible in a flexible world"**. He very rightly remarks that so much had already been written on *Hadith* and *Fiqh* that original work was not possible for the Muslim theologian's sot they started writing commentaries and explanations. It made the task of the students much more difficult because the students were now required to read the text as well as explanations and commentaries over them. Qureshi finds that Muslim education was not for masses. Another feature which he finds was that all educational activities related to Muslim education were confined to some centres located in urban area. He is of the opinion that Muslim system of education was successful and he gives as a proof the fact that a number of learned men were produced as a result of the system and they exercised influence on the non-Muslims also.

1.6.13 **Naseem Qazi** (75) has done a study on **the Concept of man in Islam** from Rajasthan University in 1985. In the process of reflective search for an organic unit of things, we tend to think and inquire about the nature of religion, God and man, and man's relation with his Creator and Social Environment. She has tried to examine the Islamic point of view distilled from the revealed Holy Book Qur'an. **Conclusion** – In the world of change, the light encased in a glass likened into a well defined star is the nearest approach to the Absolute for which Qur'an advises man to seek knowledge. The distance between the ultimate Ego and an Individual Ego is demarcated by intensity of spiritual faith of man on Allāh and the nature of his deeds. If this faith is complete, both in Iman and Ihsan man's unison with Allāh – the spiritual assimilation of Ultimate ego and Super ego is achieved. The Qur'an prescribes *Sirat-ul-Mustakim* (the straight path of goodness) to man for this unison. In order to achieve this ultimate objective, man has to organize his life by taking judicious actions for creating a just society. This just society encompasses all objects of creation. This universal order must be based on the principles of love, equality and brotherhood that are enriched in the Holy Qur'an. Finally, this is possible if man the central actor in this mission, adheres both in *iman* and action to the first divine principle of Islam, the *Kalima – La ilaha illalhu muhammadur rasulallah* (There is no God but Allāh; Muhammad is his Prophet.)

Researcher also visited **Rajasthan University** Library and tried to find out research works in the field of Islamic Education. She found that certain research works have been done in the field of Muslim women education, Madarsa education etc. in the subjects of Sociology, Philosophy and Psychology. In the field of Education the work is very few. Islamic religion and culture have also been taken into consideration, but Educational Implications of Qur'an and *Hadith* has been untouched. That is the reason researcher has selected this topic so as to find out the role of Qur'an and *Hadith* in the development of students, teachers and society.

1.7 Statement of the Problem

"Educational Implications of Qur'an".

1.8 Definition of Technical Terms

Education—Etymologically, "**to educate**" means "**to lead out**" or "**to bring out**". Man has been endowed with many capabilities, but most of them remain dormant or embryonic until something awakens them, nourishes them and "brings them out" for a full play, Education, therefore, stands for bringing out and developing to their full potential all the faculties that are latent in each individual. Among the inherent capabilities of man there are some which, if not checked properly, have the tendency to disintegrate human personality. Education is thus bringing out and directing towards a harmonious flow all human capabilities for an individually and socially valuable, not pernicious end. This process cannot be left to chance or experiences of trial and error, for that would mean chaos and disorderliness amounting a denial or man's own faculties of setting things right. Man, therefore, needs an artificial or '**contrived**' education in addition to that which he receives automatically through experience.

According to **Mahatma Gandhi**,

> *"By Education I mean all round drawing the best in child and man's body, mind and soul."*

Qur'an—The Qur'an is the sacred book of the Muslims. It is seen as perfect revelation from God, a faithful reproduction of an original engraved on a tablet in heaven which has existed from all eternity. The word 'Qur'an' comes from the Arabic verb "to recite", *qara'a*. This bears out the fact that most of the book is in the form of the words of Allāh which Muhammad (SAW) was commanded to proclaim. After 1st chapter, Qur'an consists of 14 chapters (*suras*). These are arranged according to length, the longest near the beginning, and the shortest at the end. Allāh, the Exalted, revealed the Qur'an, to be a beacon of light that cannot be extinguished. It is a methodology and way of life that is perfect in all respects. In it is strength that cannot be equaled or repelled. The Book of Allāh to mankind's guidance is like the soul in relation to the body.

Hadith – Reports on the sayings and the traditions of Prophet Muhammad (SAW) or what he witnessed and approved are called *Hadith*. These are the real explanations, interpretations and the living example of the Prophet (SAW) for teachings of Qur'an. His sayings are found in books called the *Hadith* Books. Some famous collectors of *Hadith* are Imam Al-Bukhari, Imam Muslim, Imam An-Nasri, Imam At-Tirmizi, there are many others.

1.9 Emerging Questions from the Study

Q. 1 How can the study of Qur'an helpful in Education?
Q. 2 How can the study of Qur'an helpful in the development of students?
Q. 3 How can the study of Qur'an be beneficial for Teachers?
Q. 4 How can the study of Qur'an be beneficial for Society?
Q. 5 What the guidance given in Qur'an is helpful for the improvement of Society?

1.10 Objectives

1. To study guidance and preaching of Prophet which could be helpful for students.
2. To study duties and characteristics of the Teacher mentioned in the Qur'an and *Hadith*.
3. To study the role of Qur'an and Preaching of Prophet for the benefit of Society.
4. To study the Educational Implications of Qur'an and *Hadith*.

1.11 Research Methodology

The research methodology used is **Philosophical**. The method employed in this study consists of:

- Reviewing the literature available on the Islamic Education, on the Philosophy of Qur'an, teachings of Qur'an, history of Qur'an or the background of Qur'an.
- Reviewing the Qur'an and its translations.

1.12 Justification of the Problem

There is very intimate relation between religion and education. Education broadens human outlook. It tries to modify human behaviour according to those ideals and values which are recognized by religion as of worth and importance. Every religion is based on some sacred and holy books which give its followers guidelines, duties, values as divine commandments. **Study of those holy books and education aim at the wholesome and fullest development of human personality which includes mental as well as spiritual development.** We see that in ancient times religious persons were teachers also. Likewise **Prophet Mohammad (SAW) was a teacher, preacher and a guide** of Islamic Society. They taught children to discharge their duties and society both and thus developed their personality to the full so that they were able to lead their lives happily and peacefully.

The Qura'n which is religious book of Islam contains the word of God. The Holy Qur'an claims to be Book of Hidaya, i.e. Guidance, for man. It is the essence of all the messages sent down in the past. **It has depicted a path, the straight path which when followed revolutionize the whole of life**. It brings about a transformation in character and galvanizes us into action and this action takes the form of purification of the self. Reports of Prophets Sayings and deeds are called as *Hadith*s. Preaching's of Prophet Mohammad and the guidance of Qur'an is like an ocean, wide and infinite. Researcher has tried to find out the Educational Implications of Qur'an and *Hadith*.

As we have seen in the related literature various researches have been done related to Qur'an and Islam. Maximum of the researches are **survey work**, in the field of Sociology, philosophy etc. Previous studies are based basically on the improvement of the Muslim education. It is because Muslims are very much backward related in case of education, especially in women education. So, these works emphasize on the change of curriculum, syllabus, methods etc. They show real picture of Muslims and encourage them to wake up and move towards education for their overall development. Very little work has been done, particularly in the field of Education. Researcher also visited Rajasthan University Library and tried to find out research works in the field of Islamic Education. She found that certain research works have been done in the field of Muslim women education, Madarsa education etc. in the subjects of Sociology, Philosophy and Psychology. Islamic religion and culture have also been taken into consideration, but Educational Implications of Qur'an and *Hadith* has been untouched. However, the study done by Ansari is very detailed and good study. He has considered philosophy of Qur'an in Islamic culture. His research is a Historical research. Various points of my study match with this study. But my research is a philosophical research. Various comparisons have also been done comparison of *Gita* and *Qur'an*, Bible and Qur'an etc. The researcher has selected this topic so as to find out the role of Qur'an and *Hadith* in the development of students, teachers and society. Besides these, Rizvi has also written on the importance Islamic Education for the society and the teachers. Shalabi has also concentrated on the importance of Islamic education for teachers. But still students are not taken into consideration. Researcher has focused upon teachers, students and society. Researcher did not find any research in Rajasthan University as well as in Buch Surveys which highlights Educational Implications of Qur'an and *Hadith*.

Researcher wants to depict significance of Qur'an and *Hadith* for students, teachers and society. How can the guidance of Qur'an and preaching of Prophet Mohammad can be beneficial for the students, teachers and our society, this is the objective of the present research. Looking at the present day man, one is constrained to believe that he is almost devoid of all the basic virtues which characterize man for whom the universe has been brought into being. The modern man has axed the real man within him, while he himself is making frantic efforts to catch at something which may satisfy his unjustified and ever increasing greed and passion. The world is moving on the wheels of time at a terrific speed. There is no doubt that man has set his foot on the moon and hoisted a flag of his victory over there; yet there are thousands of stars and galaxies to be explored which may be virtually far beyond the slipknot of his lasso. Inspite of the new adventures and discoveries man is shaky and fretful. **Human values have degenerated deplorably and the real man is becoming extinct**. An unseen danger is always lurking ahead. Obviously, we are treading along a wrong route of life. Being conscious of the weaknesses of the modern education which has become predominantly secular, intellectually too heavy and inapprehensible, I thought **we might make a recourse to the Holy Qur'an which has come down from the Creator for the guidance of mankind and which provides the indicative light**. And surely it does.

The teacher is the pivot of the educational system. He is the real maker of history. He is the architect who builds, rebuilds, shapes and reshapes the psychological world of the young members of the society. Progress of the society depends considerably upon its schools. Goodness of the school is determined from the type of teachers working in it. Without good teachers, even the best of system is bound to fail. There is need of really good teachers who have some unique qualities about them. In India we donot need such teachers who consider imparting of information to be their only duty. They are also expected to act as social reformer, moralist, national integrator etc. In the present time as we know both mother and father are working, so most of the time child remains in the school. Schools are now of day-boarding type. The education which is envisaged in the Holy Qur'an is the unique code of human guidance in all the walks of life. The Qur'an deals with almost every aspect of the universe and reflects upon every basic problem of life. It is indeed the most comprehensive Book—the source of all information and inspiration—required to be followed by man to complete his mission of life by individual and collective endeavour. The child in his early infancy is governed by certain laws of nature. He will develop properly if he is educated in the light of those laws. He has a natural tendency to accept what is pleasant, brilliant and attractive, and responds favourably to expressions of love and affection. He needs education which conforms to his inherent attitudes and natural propensities.

The last Prophet of Islam Muhammad (SAW) was an educationist and a teacher in the widest and truest sense of the world. He was a teacher par-excellence. He remained a teacher all through his life. He taught his people the basic values of the new civilization the he was establishing. He taught them Islam; he taught his followers all that they needed for the betterment of this life and the life hereafter. And all this was achieved, not through preaching alone, but also through the example of his practice. The teacher in a society is an element of social change. He should be motivated by the general instruction of the prophet. Thus, **the study of Qur'an and *Hadith* would be very beneficial for the teachers, students and thus for the whole society**. Let the world adhere to the teachings of the Qur'an which are unquestionably genuine and beneficial, when all other instruction has failed in making the human race really literate and providing peace and happiness to the world.

2
Content of the Qur'an

2.1 The Background of Qur'an

The Qur'an (also spelled Koran, Qur'an, Al-Koran etc.) is a Message from Allāh to humanity. It was transmitted to us in a chain starting from the Almighty Himself (SWT) to the angel Gabriel to the Prophet Muhammad (SAW). This message was given to the Prophet (SAW) in pieces over a period spanning approximately 23 years (610 to 622). The Prophet (SAW) was 40 years old when the Qur'an began to be revealed to him, and he was 63 when the revelation was completed. The language of the original message was Arabic, but it has been translated into many other languages. The Qur'an is one leg of two which form the basis of Islam. The second leg is the *Sunnah* of the Prophet (SAW). Ater his first vision in 610 A.D., up until his death in 632, Muhammad (SAW) prophesied from time to time in a kind of trance. These pronouncements, in the Arabic language, dealt with many subjects such as: God's prophets and scriptures, God's mercy and punishment, death, the Last Day, good and evil spirits, laws of marriage, divorce, warfare, and so on. When Muhammad prophesied, his followers learnt the words by heart, or wrote them down on stones, bones, palm leaves etc. (for paper was scarce in those days). Finally, all these pronouncements were collected and edited in a single book— there is some difference of opinion among Muslims as to whether this editing was completed before or after the death of the Prophet. It is this collection of pronouncements which we know as the **Qur'an**—the word 'Qur'an' literally means **proclamation** or **recitation**.

But Muslims go much further than this. They believe that these are the words of God Himself, spoken through the lips of His Prophet, but not in any way coming from the mind and experience of Muhammad. They believe that the **"mother of the Qur'an" (ummu-l-kitab)** is in heaven, written by God Himself on a **"guarded tablet" (lawhu-l-mahfuz);** and that the angel Gabriel brought the tablet down to Muhammad -- so that the Qur'an which we have today is a copy of the "guarded tablet" in heaven. It is an obligation—and blessing—for all who hear of the Qur'an and Islam to investigate it and evaluate it for themselves. Allāh has guaranteed that He will protect the Qur'an from human tampering, and today's readers can find exact copies of it all over the world. The Qur'an of today is the same as the Qur'an revealed to Muhammad (SAW). The Qur'an is the sacred book of the Muslims. It is seen as perfect relevation from God, a faithful reproduction of an original engraved on a tablet in heaven which has existed from all eternity.

The word **Qur'an** comes from the Arabic verb '**to recite**', **qara'a**. This bears out the fact that most of the book is in the form of the words of Allāh which Muhammad (SAW) was commanded to proclaim. The Holy Qur'an claims to be **Book of Hidyahay, i.e. Guidance, for man**. It is a Book that is available to all mankind –indeed it addresses itself, by and large, to the totality of mankind. Its message is relevant to different peoples living in different parts of the world. Further, its message is valid for all times to come – in other words, it is not a Book that will ever be out of date. The Qur'an as a Book of Guidance has itself commented upon full implication of the concept of Hidayah. Hidayah literally means '***to guide***' and '***to show the way***'. In *Surah al-Ala* of the Qur'an reference is made to all the relevant aspects of the process of development through which all created beings pass.

> *"Praise the name of the Lord, the Most High, who has created and then equliberated all things, Who has appointed*

their destinies and Who has guided them" (al-Qur'an 87:1-2)

The meaning of Sura and Aya: ***Sura*** means a "chapter" of the Qur'an. There are 114 *suras*, and Muslims generally refer to them by the name given to each one, rather than by number. These are arranged according to length, the longest near the beginning, the shortest at the end. They are a composite collection of verses written at various periods of Mohammad Saheb's life.

The *suras* are divided into verses (*ayat*). ***Aya*** means literally a "**sign**", and so a part of the Qur'an, generally one verse. The word *ayat* also carries the meaning of 'a miracle'. When Prophet Muhammad (SAW) was asked for an authentic wonder to prove his prophetic role, he simply referred to the Qur'an and its verses; they were his miracle. Estimates differ, but there are commonly said to be 6,247 verses, 77,934 words and 3,23,621 letters in the Qur'an. To give an idea of its length, the Qur'an is a little shorter shorter than the NewTestament. For recitation the Qur'an is divided into 60 sections, known as "**hizb**", which do not correspond at all with the chapter divisions.

In this Book, the Holy Prophet's life, the history of the Arabs and the events which occurred during the period of the revelation of the Qur'an have not been mingled with the Divine Verses, as is the case with the Bible. **The Qur'an is the pure word of God**. Not one word therein is not divine. Not a single word has been deleted from its text. The Book has been handed down to our age in its complete and original form since the time of Prophet Muhammad. From the time the Book began to be revealed, the Holy Prophet had dictated its text to the scribes. Whenever some Divine Message was revealed, the Holy Prophet would call a scribe and dictate its words to him. The written text was then read out to the Holy Prophet, who, having satisfied himself that the scribe has committed no error of recording, would put the manuscript in safe custody. The Holy Prophet used to instruct the scribe about the sequence in which a revealed message was to be placed in a particular *Surah* (chapter). In this manner, the Holy Prophet continued to arrange the text of the

Qur'an in systematic order till the end of the chain of revelations. Again, it was ordained from the beginning of Islam that a recitation of the Holy Qur'an must be an integral part of worship. Hence, the illustrious Companions would commit the Divine *verses* to memory as soon as they were revealed. Many of them learned the whole text and a far larger number had memorized different portions of it.

2.2 Social and Political Background of Qur'an

At the turn of 7th century Mecca was the most important commercial city in the Hijaz, at the cross-roads of two important caravan routes. One route went from Yemen to Syria and the other from Iraq to Abyssinia. It also housed the Kabaa, the place of worship Prophet Abraham (PBUH) built several thousand years ago. It provided a sanctuary where people came from far distances without fear. These two factors played an important part in the growth of Mecca into a prosperous trading centre and an important financial hub, whose leading men where skillful in credit, investment and speculation. As a result, they had their financial influence as far as Yemen, Syria and Iraq. Mecca was the home of tribe of Quraysh. Only two generations ago they had lived a tough nomadic life, which required a grim struggle for daily survival. The *surah* or chapter 106—The Quraysh is addressed to the tribe of Quraysh and reminds them of the bounties of God (Allāh) who gave them provisions and peace through their caravan trade and house of God. Due to Kabba and the caravan trade the Meccan grew rich beyond their wildest dreams. Yet their drastically altered lifestyle meant that the old tribal values had been superseded by a rampant and ruthless capitalism. As a result the situation in Mecca was that of decline. This is the social background in which the primary message of Qur'an was first revealed.

2.3 About *Hadith*

Hadith are traditions relating to the **words and deeds of Muhammad**. *Hadith* collections are regarded as important tools for determining the *Sunnah*, or Muslim way of life, by all traditional schools of jurisprudence. A *hadith* was originally an oral tradition relevant to the actions and customs of the Islamic prophet Muhammad. Starting the first Islamic civil war of the 7th century, those receiving the *hadith* started to question the sources of the saying. This resulted in a chain of transmission, for example "A told me that B told him that Muhammad said". The *hadith* were eventually recorded in written form, had their chain of transmission recorded and were collected into large collections mostly during the reign of Umar II during 8th century, something that solidified in the 9th century. These works are still today referred to in matters of Islamic law and history.

The overwhelming majority of Muslims consider *hadith* to be essential supplements to and clarifications of the Qur'an, Islam's holy book. In Islamic jurisprudence, the Qur'an contains many rules for the behaviour expected of Muslims. However, there are many matters of concern, both religious and practical, on which there are no specific Qur'anic rules. Muslims believe that they can look at the way of life, or *sunnah*, of Muhammad and his companions to discover what to imitate and what to avoid. Muslim scholars also find it useful to know how Muhammad or his companions explained the revelations, or upon what occasion Muhammad received them. Sometimes this will clarify a passage that otherwise seems obscure. *Hadith* are a source for Islamic history and biography. For the vast majority of devout Muslims, authentic *hadith* are also a source of religious inspiration. However, some contemporary Muslims argue that the Qur'an alone is sufficient.

Knowledge of *hadith* is essential in an effort to understand Islam. They contain rules and regulations, when implemented, would give cause to a better understanding of everyday life. This is applicable, to the individual of a society and also to the society as a whole. The messages within the *ahadith* are for the benefit of both, individual and society. The Qur'an was revealed to the Last Messenger Muhammad (SAW) through the angel Gabriel. The *ahadith* show us the diversities a single person can have, and the ways these diversities may be used to produce an optimal performance, where the performance is exemplary for future generations. This was one of the main tasks of the Last Messenger (peace be upon him), to guide humanity on the right path. Muhammad (peace be upon him) was a son, a husband, a father, an advisor, a warrior, a leader, a judge and most important of all, he was the Seal of the Prophets—the last messenger of Allāh. A man with such a character and such a vast field of responsibility is indeed deserving of biographical study, and through the ages, biographical researches have been carried out. The collection of *ahadith* is the result of these researchers. The study of *ahadith* is a science itself.

2.4 Moral Values in the Holy Qur'an

From the educational point of view, all social behaviour must emanate from the permanent values of life given by the Holy Qur'an; because Education itself is a continuous process in which the present generation of human beings pases on to its next future generation human beings passes on to its next future generation not only skills and attitudes, but also values beyond material goods. Thus, the permanent values of life from the nucleus of the Qur'anic educational philosophy round which all educational activities must revolve, right from the elementary to the final stage of schooling.

The aim of human life, as also the purpose of education, is to develop as muc as possible these attributes in every human personality. When a child is lacking in certain attribute, the teacher has it cultivate it in him through various educational means. It is impossible to enumerate and explain in detail all the Qur'anic Universals, so I shall confine them to explaining only those universals which have a direct bearing on the educational philosophy:

2.4.1 Tauhidur Rabubiyat

Nourishing-Sustaining-Evolving attribute of Allāh is the first permanent value which we human beings must develop and perpetuate in ourselves. This permanent value is, in fact, the actualization of man's latent potentialities; hence, it forms the very base of the whole of our educational structure. The human 'self' is to be so perfected, individually as well as collectively, within the limitations of its possibilities that it is fitly able to carry out its responsibilities of developing and nourishing the entire mankind on principles of love and sympathy, mercy and benevolence, cordiality and kindness.

الصَّابِرِينَ وَالصَّادِقِينَ وَالْقَانِتِينَ وَالْمُنْفِقِينَ وَالْمُسْتَغْفِرِينَ بِالأَسْحَارِ.

Those who show patience, Firmness and self-control; who are true (in word and deed); who worship devoutly; who spend (in the way of Allāh); and who pray for forgiveness in the early hours of the morning. [Al-Qur'an, 003.017, Aal-E-Imran (The Family of Imran)].

2.4.2 Bearing Duties and Responsibilities

To be responsible means to bear one's own burden, to accept open heartedly the consequences of exercising free-will. Freedom of the will has a relationship with the dignity of man also. Through the exercise of free-will he is enabled to build his individual life and create his particular character as he wishes. He must, at the same time, feely morally responsible to accept his weaknesses and failures. This moral courage gives extra strength to man's personality and a big step towards self-correction and repentance. Justice also demands that only those actions be considered punishable that flow from a free and deliberate choice.

وَمَنْ يَكْسِبْ إِثْمًا فَإِنَّمَا يَكْسِبُهُ عَلَى نَفْسِهِ وَكَانَ اللَّهُ عَلِيمًا حَكِيمً

And if any one earns sin, he earns it against His own soul: for Allāh is full of knowledge and wisdom. [Al-Qur'an, 004.111, An-Nisa (Women)]

وَمَنْ يَكْسِبْ خَطِيئَةً أَوْ إِثْمًا ثُمَّ يَرْمِ بِهِ بَرِيئًا فَقَدِ احْتَمَلَ بُهْتَانًا وَإِثْمًا مُبِينًا

But if any one earns a fault or a sin and throws it on to one that is innocent, He carries (on himself) (Both) a falsehood and a flagrant sin. [Al-Qur'an, 004.112, An-Nisa (Women)]

2.4.3. Fulfillment of Promises and Agreement

Fulfilment of promises and agreements is another permanent value of the Holy Qur'an. A covenant is to be looked upon as a solemn undertaking. One must not enter into an agreement of one thinks that its carrying out by him, will be doubtful in future. Breaking of agreements is an unpardonable sin. In international politics, too, there cannot be any relaxation.

وَإِذْ أَخَذْنَا مِيثَاقَ بَنِي إِسْرَائِيلَ لا تَعْبُدُونَ إِلا اللهَ وَبِالْوَالِدَيْنِ إِحْسَانًا وَذِي
الْقُرْبَى وَالْيَتَامَى وَالْمَسَاكِينِ وَقُولُوا لِلنَّاسِ حُسْنًا وَأَقِيمُوا الصَّلاةَ وَآتُوا
الزَّكَاةَ ثُمَّ تَوَلَّيْتُمْ إِلا قَلِيلا مِنْكُمْ وَأَنْتُمْ مُعْرِضُونَ

And remember We took a covenant from the Children of Israel (to this effect): Worship none but Allāh; treat with kindness your parents and kindred, and orphans and those in need; speak fair to the people; be steadfast in prayer; and practise regular charity. Then did ye turn back, except a few among you, and ye backslide (even now). [Al-Qur'an, 002.083, Al-Baqara (The Cow)]

وَالَّذِينَ يَنْقُضُونَ عَهْدَ اللهِ مِنْ بَعْدِ مِيثَاقِهِ وَيَقْطَعُونَ مَا أَمَرَ اللهُ بِهِ أَنْ
يُوصَلَ وَيُفْسِدُونَ فِي الأَرْضِ أُولَئِكَ لَهُمُ اللَّعْنَةُ وَلَهُمْ سُوءُ الدَّارِ

But those who break the Covenant of Allāh, after having plighted their word thereto, and cut asunder those things which Allāh has commanded to be joined, and work mischief in the land; on them is the curse; for them is the terrible home! [Al-Qur'an, 013.025, Ar-Rad (The Thunder)]

2.4.4. Justice

In a society in which justice is not practiced in daily affairs nothing remains in its proper place. Qur'anic justice is something higher than that conceived by human law. In committing good or bad acts the believer is ardently sure that he constantly being watched by Allāh and that all his actions and motives are known to Him. He believes that Allāh knows "even the finest mischiefs that the eyes make and the secret thoughts that pass in the mind." Justice is therefore, the highest quality for which a Muslim has to stand firm as a witness of Allāh, even if it be against one's personal interests or against the interests of his dear and near ones.

يَا أَيُّهَا الَّذِينَ آمَنُوا كُونُوا قَوَّامِينَ لِلَّهِ شُهَدَاءَ بِالْقِسْطِ وَلَا يَجْرِمَنَّكُمْ شَنَآنُ قَوْمٍ عَلَى أَلَّا تَعْدِلُوا اعْدِلُوا هُوَ أَقْرَبُ لِلتَّقْوَى وَاتَّقُوا اللَّهَ إِنَّ اللَّهَ خَبِيرٌ بِمَا تَعْمَلُونَ

O ye who believe! stand out firmly for Allāh, as witnesses to fair dealing, and let not the hatred of others to you make you swerve to wrong and depart from justice. Be just: that is next to piety: and fear Allāh. For Allāh is well-acquainted with all that ye do. [Al-Qur'an, 005.008, Al-Maeda (The Table, The Table Spread)]

يَعِدُهُمْ وَيُمَنِّيهِمْ وَمَا يَعِدُهُمُ الشَّيْطَانُ إِلَّا غُرُورًا

Satan makes them promises, and creates in them false desires; but satan's promises are nothing but deception. [Al-Qur'an, 004.120, An-Nisa (Women)]

يَا أَيُّهَا الَّذِينَ آمَنُوا كُونُوا قَوَّامِينَ بِالْقِسْطِ شُهَدَاءَ لِلَّهِ وَلَوْ عَلَى أَنْفُسِكُمْ أَوِ الْوَالِدَيْنِ وَالْأَقْرَبِينَ إِنْ يَكُنْ غَنِيًّا أَوْ فَقِيرًا فَاللَّهُ أَوْلَى بِهِمَا فَلَا تَتَّبِعُوا الْهَوَى أَنْ تَعْدِلُوا وَإِنْ تَلْوُوا أَوْ تُعْرِضُوا فَإِنَّ اللَّهَ كَانَ بِمَا تَعْمَلُونَ خَبِيرًا

O ye who believe! stand out firmly for justice, as witnesses to Allāh, even as against yourselves, or your parents, or your kin, and whether it be (against) rich or poor: for Allāh can best protect both. Follow not the lusts (of your hearts), lest ye swerve, and if ye distort (justice) or decline to do justice, verily Allāh is well-acquainted with all that ye do. [Al-Qur'an, 004.135, An-Nisa (Women)]

2.4.5. Virtuousness

Beauty (in Arabic **'Husn'**, from which the world Ihsan, meaning setting things right, has been derived) has no other meaning that corrects proportion and right relationship between the parts that constitute the whole. Creating beauty in a society is, therefore, nothing else than giving freely to those who need it, from no other motive than love.

وَلا تَسْتَوِي الْحَسَنَةُ وَلا السَّيِّئَةُ ادْفَعْ بِالَّتِي هِيَ أَحْسَنُ فَإِذَا الَّذِي بَيْنَكَ وَبَيْنَهُ عَدَاوَةٌ كَأَنَّهُ وَلِيٌّ حَمِيمٌ

Nor can goodness and Evil be equal. Repel (Evil) with what is better: Then will he between whom and thee was hatred become as it were thy friend and intimate! [Al-Qur'an, 041.034, Fussilat (Explained in Detail)]

وَمَا يُلَقَّاهَا إِلا الَّذِينَ صَبَرُوا وَمَا يُلَقَّاهَا إِلا ذُو حَظٍّ عَظِيمٍ

And no one will be granted such goodness except those who exercise patience and self-restraint,—none but persons of the greatest good fortune. [Al-Qur'an, 041.035 (Fussilat)]

2.4.6. Dispensation of Wealth

This is the basic principles on which stands the most unshakable structure of the economic system of the Muslims. This value is called "Infaq" by the Holy Qur'an. Infaq means spending, disbursement simply to please God without asking for any favour or hoping for return. It has the idea of ever-busy inlets and oulests of material goods as in a flourishing market which keeps wealth constantly in circulation. Giving away goods to the needy is establishing truth in the eyes of the Holy Qur'an and, therefore, it is a permanent value.

Charity has been praised as virtue by all the religions of the world. It has been practiced by humanity for centuries. But individual charity in the shape of giving alms to the poor by wealthy persons has always brought degradation to man and injured his self-respect. The Qura'n which liberates human beings from all slaveries cannot, tolerate any such custom. In every society there are men who are forced by uncontrollable circumstances to stand in need of other's help. The Holy Qur'an says that Honourable andpermanent means of subsistence must be provided to them through a legalized institution. The Muslim must directly be charged with this responsibility.

لِلْفُقَرَاءِ الَّذِينَ أُحْصِرُوا فِي سَبِيلِ اللَّهِ لا يَسْتَطِيعُونَ ضَرْبًا فِي الأَرْضِ يَحْسَبُهُمُ الْجَاهِلُ أَغْنِيَاءَ مِنَ التَّعَفُّفِ تَعْرِفُهُمْ بِسِيمَاهُمْ لا يَسْأَلُونَ النَّاسَ إِلْحَافًا وَمَا تُنْفِقُوا مِنْ خَيْرٍ فَإِنَّ اللَّهَ بِهِ عَلِيمٌ

(Charity is) for those in need, who, in Allāh's cause are restricted (from travel), and cannot move about in the land, seeking (For trade or work): the ignorant man thinks, because of their modesty, that they are free from want. Thou shalt know them by their (Unfailing) mark: They beg not importunately from the entire sundry. And whatever of good ye give, be assured Allāh knoweth it well. [Al-Qur'an, 002.273, Al-Baqara (The Cow)]

Charity has value only if that thing is given away which is (1) good and useful, (2) which has lawfully been earned and honourably acquired by the giver and (3) which is produced in Nature as a bounty of Allāh.

يَا أَيُّهَا الَّذِينَ آمَنُوا أَنْفِقُوا مِنْ طَيِّبَاتِ مَا كَسَبْتُمْ وَمِمَّا أَخْرَجْنَا لَكُمْ مِنَ الأَرْضِ وَلا تَيَمَّمُوا الْخَبِيثَ مِنْهُ تُنْفِقُونَ وَلَسْتُمْ بِآخِذِيهِ إِلا أَنْ تُغْمِضُوا فِيهِ وَاعْلَمُوا أَنَّ اللَّهَ غَنِيٌّ حَمِيدٌ

O ye who believe! Give of the good things which ye have (honourably) earned, and of the fruits of the earth which We have produced for you, and do not even aim at getting anything which is bad, in order that out of it ye may give away something, when ye yourselves would not receive it except with closed eyes. And know that Allāh is Free of all wants, and worthy of all praise. [Al-Qur'an, 002.267, Al-Baqara (The Cow)]

2.4.7. Regard for Mankind

وَلَقَدْ كَرَّمْنَا بَنِي آدَمَ وَحَمَلْنَاهُمْ فِي الْبَرِّ وَالْبَحْرِ وَرَزَقْنَاهُمْ مِنَ الطَّيِّبَاتِ
وَفَضَّلْنَاهُمْ عَلَى كَثِيرٍ مِمَّنْ خَلَقْنَا تَفْضِيلا

We have honoured the sons of Adam; provided them with transport on land and sea; given them for sustenance things good and pure; and conferred on them special favours, above a great part of our creation. [Al-Qur'an, 017.070, Al-Isra (Isra, The Night Journey, Children of Israel)]

Men and women, children and adults are to be honoured not for any of their individual achievements or for their individual differences or for their belonging to a particular class or society or country but on basis of equality simply because all are the descendants of the same ancestor. Every child of Adam is Himself an Adam; therefore to lose any one child means to lose one whole generation of human beings. Respect for humanity includes reverence for women also. Allāh has laid down in the Holy Qur'an that reverence for women are considered as a permanent value of life.

2.4.8. Unification of Humanity

The Message of Allāh has always been for maintaining the unity of mankind. Differences spring up between individuals and nations through selfishness and egotism. Man has been given the faculty of reasoning, understanding and intelligence. He must, therefore, consciously strive for the unity of its own kind and patch up all differences which are born of nothing but ugly motives.

كَانَ النَّاسُ أُمَّةً وَاحِدَةً فَبَعَثَ اللَّهُ النَّبِيِّينَ مُبَشِّرِينَ وَمُنْذِرِينَ وَأَنْزَلَ الْكِتَابَ
بِالْحَقِّ لِيَحْكُمَ بَيْنَ النَّاسِ فِيمَا اخْتَلَفُوا فِيهِ وَمَا اخْتَلَفَ فِيهِ إِلا الَّذِينَ أُوتُوهُ مِنْ
بَعْدِ مَا جَاءَتْهُمُ الْبَيِّنَاتُ بَغْيًا بَيْنَهُمْ فَهَدَى اللَّهُ الَّذِينَ آمَنُوا لِمَا اخْتَلَفُوا فِيهِ مِنَ
الْحَقِّ بِإِذْنِهِ وَاللَّهُ يَهْدِي مَنْ يَشَاءُ إِلَى صِرَاطٍ مُسْتَقِيمٍ

Mankind was one single nation, and Allāh sent Messengers with glad tidings and warnings; and with them He sent the Book in truth, to judge between people in matters wherein they differed; but the People of the Book, after the clear Signs came to them, did not differ among themselves, except through selfish contumacy. Allāh by His Grace Guided the believers to the Truth, concerning that wherein they differed. For Allāh guided whom He will to a path that is straight. [Al-Qur'an, 002.213 (Al-Baqara)]

2.4.9. Knowledge and Understanding

Allāh is perfect in knowledge and wisdom. He sees all and He is all hearing and all knowing. He is full of knowledge and is acquainted with everything. His knowledge is limited less.

قَالُوا سُبْحَانَكَ لا عِلْمَ لَنَا إِلا مَا عَلَّمْتَنَا إِنَّكَ أَنْتَ الْعَلِيمُ الْحَكِيمُ

They said: "Glory to Thee, of knowledge We have none, save what Thou Hast taught us: In truth it is Thou Who art perfect in knowledge and wisdom." [Al-Qur'an, 002.032, Al-Baqara)]

إِنَّ اللَّهَ عِنْدَهُ عِلْمُ السَّاعَةِ وَيُنَزِّلُ الْغَيْثَ وَيَعْلَمُ مَا فِي الأَرْحَامِ وَمَا تَدْرِي
نَفْسٌ مَاذَا تَكْسِبُ غَدًا وَمَا تَدْرِي نَفْسٌ بِأَيِّ أَرْضٍ تَمُوتُ إِنَّ اللَّهَ عَلِيمٌ خَبِيرٌ

Verily the knowledge of the Hour is with Allāh (alone). It is He Who sends down rain, and He Who knows what is in the wombs. Nor does any one know what it is that he will earn on the morrow: Nor does any one know in what land he is to die. Verily with Allāh is full knowledge and He is acquainted (with all things). [Al-Qur'an, 031.034, Luqman (Luqman)]

Acquisition of wisdom and knowledge are permanent values to be endeared by all human beings. Those who have hearts but they understand not, have eyes but they see not, have ears wherewith they hear not, are like dumb, driven cattle, may even more misguided; for they are heedless of the warning sent to them through Allāh's final Revelation.

كَمَا أَرْسَلْنَا فِيكُمْ رَسُولًا مِنْكُمْ يَتْلُو عَلَيْكُمْ آيَاتِنَا وَيُزَكِّيكُمْ وَيُعَلِّمُكُمُ الْكِتَابَ وَالْحِكْمَةَ وَيُعَلِّمُكُمْ مَا لَمْ تَكُونُوا تَعْلَمُونَ

A similar (favour have ye already received) in that We have sent among you a Messenger of your own, rehearsing to you Our Signs, and sanctifying you, and instructing you in Scripture and Wisdom, and in new knowledge. [Al-Qur'an, 002.151, Al-Baqara)]

وَلَقَدْ جِئْنَاهُمْ بِكِتَابٍ فَصَّلْنَاهُ عَلَى عِلْمٍ هُدًى وَرَحْمَةً لِقَوْمٍ يُؤْمِنُونَ

For We had certainly sent unto them a Book, based on knowledge, which We explained in detail,—a guide and a mercy to all who believe. [Al-Qur'an, 007.052 (Al-Araf)]

تَنْزِيلُ الْكِتَابِ مِنَ اللَّهِ الْعَزِيزِ الْعَلِيمِ

The revelation of this Book is from Allāh, Exalted in Power, Full of Knowledge. [Al-Qur'an, 040.002, Al-Ghafir (The Forgiver) [God)]]

فَتَعَالَى اللَّهُ الْمَلِكُ الْحَقُّ وَلَا تَعْجَلْ بِالْقُرْآنِ مِنْ قَبْلِ أَنْ يُقْضَى إِلَيْكَ وَحْيُهُ وَقُلْ رَبِّ زِدْنِي عِلْمًا

High above all is Allāh, the King, the Truth! Be not in haste with the Qur'an before its revelation to thee is completed, but say, "O my Lord! advance me in knowledge." [Al-Qur'an, 020.114, Ta-Ha (Mystic letters Ta-Ha)]

Knowledge thus acquired leads to real faith and becomes **'power'** when it follows the right path to which the All-knowing, perfect-in-Wisdom and the most Merciful Allāh has guided.

2.4.10. Individual Effort

"First deserve, then desire', is the well-known saying that gives, in a nutshell, the whole of the philosophy of the toil and struggle of life. To achieve a goal, one has to strive constantly, persistently and with perseverance. Each one is responsible for all that he does. He must reap the crop that he sows. To sit still, in wait for something extraordinary to happen from outsides, is to invite death.

انْفِرُوا خِفَافًا وَثِقَالا وَجَاهِدُوا بِأَمْوَالِكُمْ وَأَنْفُسِكُمْ فِي سَبِيلِ اللَّهِ ذَلِكُمْ خَيْرٌ لَكُمْ إِنْ كُنْتُمْ تَعْلَمُونَ

Go ye forth, (whether equipped) lightly or heavily, and strive and struggle, with your goods and your persons, in the cause of Allāh. That is best for you, if ye (but) knew. [Al-Qur'an, 009.041, At-Tawba (Repentance, Dispensation)]

لَقَدْ خَلَقْنَا الإِنْسَانَ فِي كَبَدٍ

Verily, We have created man into toil and struggle. [Al-Qur'an, 090.004, Al-Balad (The City, This Countryside)]

2.4.11. Patience, Tolerance, Freedom of Choice

Man is free to choose between right and wrong as he wishes. Islam recognizes this freedom to the extent of a permanent value. People cannot be made to accept truth by force or co-ercion, not can ideologies be trusted upon unwilling people. Faith comes not from cumplsion but from the insight which is the natural outcome of right reasoning and clear understanding. The principle of "no compulsion entails tolerance and politeness." Islam stands for peace and security. A Muslim does not encourage or indulge in idle talk of foolish arguments about sacred things.

لا إِكْرَاهَ فِي الدِّينِ قَدْ تَبَيَّنَ الرُّشْدُ مِنَ الْغَيِّ فَمَنْ يَكْفُرْ بِالطَّاغُوتِ وَيُؤْمِنْ بِاللَّهِ فَقَدِ اسْتَمْسَكَ بِالْعُرْوَةِ الْوُثْقَى لا انْفِصَامَ لَهَا وَاللَّهُ سَمِيعٌ عَلِيمٌ

Let there be no compulsion in religion: Truth stands out clear from Error: whoever rejects evil and believes in Allāh hath grasped the most trustworthy hand-hold, that never breaks. And Allāh heareth and knoweth all things. [Al-Qur'an, 002.256, Al-Baqara (The Cow)]

إِنَّ الْمُسْلِمِينَ وَالْمُسْلِمَاتِ وَالْمُؤْمِنِينَ وَالْمُؤْمِنَاتِ وَالْقَانِتِينَ وَالْقَانِتَاتِ وَالصَّادِقِينَ وَالصَّادِقَاتِ وَالصَّابِرِينَ وَالصَّابِرَاتِ وَالْخَاشِعِينَ وَالْخَاشِعَاتِ وَالْمُتَصَدِّقِينَ وَالْمُتَصَدِّقَاتِ وَالصَّائِمِينَ وَالصَّائِمَاتِ وَالْحَافِظِينَ فُرُوجَهُمْ وَالْحَافِظَاتِ وَالذَّاكِرِينَ اللَّهَ كَثِيرًا وَالذَّاكِرَاتِ أَعَدَّ اللَّهُ لَهُمْ مَغْفِرَةً وَأَجْرًا عَظِيمًا

For Muslim men and women,—for believing men and women, for devout men and women, for true men and women, for men and women who are patient and constant, for men and women who humble themselves, for men and women who give in Charity, for men and women who fast (and deny themselves), for men and women who guard their chastity, and for men and women who engage much in Allāh's praise,—for them has Allāh prepared forgiveness and great reward. [Al-Qur'an, 033.035, Al-Ahzab (The Clans, the Coalition, the Combined Forces)]

2.4.12 Purity/Celebacy

Spotless purity in thought, word and deed concerning one's self and concerning others is also a permanent value. The Holy Qur'an commands sex purity for both men and women, at all times; i.e. before marriage, during marriage and after the dissolution of the marriage. Those guilty of illicit practices are shut out of the marriage circle of chaste men and women.

الْيَوْمَ أُحِلَّ لَكُمُ الطَّيِّبَاتُ وَطَعَامُ الَّذِينَ أُوتُوا الْكِتَابَ حِلٌّ لَكُمْ وَطَعَامُكُمْ حِلٌّ لَهُمْ وَالْمُحْصَنَاتُ مِنَ الْمُؤْمِنَاتِ وَالْمُحْصَنَاتُ مِنَ الَّذِينَ أُوتُوا الْكِتَابَ مِنْ قَبْلِكُمْ إِذَا آتَيْتُمُوهُنَّ أُجُورَهُنَّ مُحْصِنِينَ غَيْرَ مُسَافِحِينَ وَلَا مُتَّخِذِي أَخْدَانٍ وَمَنْ يَكْفُرْ بِالْإِيمَانِ فَقَدْ حَبِطَ عَمَلُهُ وَهُوَ فِي الْآخِرَةِ مِنَ الْخَاسِرِينَ

This day are (all) things good and pure made lawful unto you. The food of the People of the Book is lawful unto you and yours is lawful unto them. (Lawful unto you in marriage) are (not only) chaste women who are believers, but chaste women among the People of the Book, revealed before your time,— when ye give them their due dowers, and desire chastity, not lewdness, nor secret intrigues if any one rejects faith, fruitless is his work, and in the Hereafter he will be in the ranks of those who have lost (all spiritual good). [Al-Qur'an, 005.005, Al-Maeda (The Table, The Table Spread)]

وَالَّتِي أَحْصَنَتْ فَرْجَهَا فَنَفَخْنَا فِيهَا مِنْ رُوحِنَا وَجَعَلْنَاهَا وَابْنَهَا آيَةً لِلْعَالَمِينَ

And (remember) her who guarded her chastity: We breathed into her of Our spirit, and We made her and her son a sign for all peoples. [Al-Qur'an, 021.091, Al-Anbiya (The Prophets)]

2.4.13 Proper Usage of Wealth

Full utilization of the endless bounties provided freely by Allāh for a balanced, peaceful, and prosperous life of all men on the earth. The utility goods are to be shared on basis of equality between 'haves' and the 'have nots'. Misuse of wealth (in all inclusive extensive meanings) and of the resources that bring this wealth is condemned repeatedly by the Holy Qur'an in three ways: (1) Nothing is to be acquired by wrongful means or on false pretences, individually or collectively (indulging all means of its production); (2) Wealth is not to be hoarded, amassed or held back from universal circulation, but is to be utilized freely for the good of individuals and nations on the basis of equality irrespective of who produces it and who owns it, because the real owner is Allāh and the will of the owner is to be carried out always and under all circumstances; (3) This wealth, on which rests the prosperity of the entire humanity, must not be wasted in idle pursuits; it must fructify for the common good of the people.

الْمَالُ وَالْبَنُونَ زِينَةُ الْحَيَاةِ الدُّنْيَا وَالْبَاقِيَاتُ الصَّالِحَاتُ خَيْرٌ عِنْدَ رَبِّكَ ثَوَابًا وَخَيْرٌ أَمَلًا

Wealth and sons are allurements of the life of this world: But the things that endure, good deeds, are best in the sight of thy Lord, as rewards, and best as (the foundation for) hopes. [Al-Qur'an, 018.046, Al-Kahf (The Cave)]

2.5 Some Rights and Duties

A right may be defined as a thing to which one is entitled, or privilege or immunity to which a person has a fair claim or justification. A thing that is morally good or just or proper or that is required by equality or duty may be called one's right. The Holy Qur'an is the first Charter of Liberty ever given to mankind. It breaks to pieces all the chains and fetters that powerful demagogues are wont to put on the masses under one pretext or the other. It enjoins the Islamic Socio-religious order to secure and protect these rights which are the basic minimum obligations to be fulfilled by all human beings irrespective of their caste, creed, colour, country, occupation or any such arbitrary differentiation.

The Qur'anic human rights are directly linked with the permanent values of life. It is a peculiarity of the Holy Qur'an that it not only repeats the basic virtues of morality but gives us something more also. These rights which the Holy Qur'an recognizes are those rights to which every human being is entitled simply because he is a human being, or the chosen one of Allāh, raised above most of His Creation in honour and dignity. These rights can be demanded by all men and women as their due not favour. The basic minimum rights may be enumerated as follows:

2.5.1. High Regard for Mankind

وَلَقَدْ كَرَّمْنَا بَنِي آدَمَ وَحَمَلْنَاهُمْ فِي الْبَرِّ وَالْبَحْرِ وَرَزَقْنَاهُمْ مِنَ الطَّيِّبَاتِ
وَفَضَّلْنَاهُمْ عَلَى كَثِيرٍ مِمَّنْ خَلَقْنَا تَفْضِيلًا

We have **honoured the sons of Adam**; provided them with transport on land and sea; given them for sustenance things good and pure; and conferred on them special favours, above a great part of our creation. [Al-Qur'an, 017.070, Al-Isra, (Isra, The Night Journey, Children of Israel)]

2.5.2. Gender Equality

إِنَّ الْمُسْلِمِينَ وَالْمُسْلِمَاتِ وَالْمُؤْمِنِينَ وَالْمُؤْمِنَاتِ وَالْقَانِتِينَ وَالْقَانِتَاتِ
وَالصَّادِقِينَ وَالصَّادِقَاتِ وَالصَّابِرِينَ وَالصَّابِرَاتِ وَالْخَاشِعِينَ وَالْخَاشِعَاتِ

وَالْمُتَصَدِّقِينَ وَالْمُتَصَدِّقَاتِ وَالصَّائِمِينَ وَالصَّائِمَاتِ وَالْحَافِظِينَ فُرُوجَهُمْ وَالْحَافِظَاتِ وَالذَّاكِرِينَ اللَّهَ كَثِيرًا وَالذَّاكِرَاتِ أَعَدَّ اللَّهُ لَهُمْ مَغْفِرَةً وَأَجْرًا عَظِيمًا

For Muslim men and women,—for believing men and women, for devout men and women, for true men and women, for men and women who are patient and constant, for men and women who humble themselves, for men and women who give in Charity, for men and women who fast (and deny themselves), for men and women who guard their chastity, and for men and women who engage much in Allāh's praise, for them has Allāh prepared forgiveness and great reward. [Al-Qur'an, 033.035, Al-Ahzab (The Clans, the Coalition, the Combined Forces)]

2.5.3. No Injustice to Anyone and Honour and Respect to the Righteous

وَلِكُلٍّ دَرَجَاتٌ مِمَّا عَمِلُوا وَلِيُوَفِّيَهُمْ أَعْمَالَهُمْ وَهُمْ لَا يُظْلَمُونَ

And to all are (assigned) degrees according to the deeds which they (have done), and in order that (Allāh) may recompense their deeds, and no injustice be done to them. [Al-Qur'an, 046.019, Al-Ahqaf (The Wind-curved Sandhills, The Dunes)]

يَا أَيُّهَا النَّاسُ إِنَّا خَلَقْنَاكُمْ مِنْ ذَكَرٍ وَأُنْثَى وَجَعَلْنَاكُمْ شُعُوبًا وَقَبَائِلَ لِتَعَارَفُوا إِنَّ أَكْرَمَكُمْ عِنْدَ اللَّهِ أَتْقَاكُمْ إِنَّ اللَّهَ عَلِيمٌ خَبِيرٌ

O mankind! We created you from a single (pair) of a male and a female, and made you into nations and tribes, that ye may know each other (not that ye may despise (each other). Verily, the most honoured of you in the sight of Allāh is (he who is) the most righteous of you. And Allāh has full knowledge and is well acquainted (with all things). (Al-Qur'an, 049.013, Al-Hujraat (The Private Apartments, The Inner Apartments)]

2.5.4. To Every Soul will be Paid, in Full, the Earnings of His "Deeds"

وَوُفِّيَتْ كُلُّ نَفْسٍ مَا عَمِلَتْ وَهُوَ أَعْلَمُ بِمَا يَفْعَلُونَ

And to every soul will be paid in full (the fruit) of its Deeds; and (Allāh) knoweth best all that they do. (Al-Qur'an, 039.070, Az-Zumar (The Troops, Throngs)]

2.5.5. Justice to All

إِنَّ اللَّهَ يَأْمُرُ بِالْعَدْلِ وَالإِحْسَانِ وَإِيتَاءِ ذِي الْقُرْبَى وَيَنْهَى عَنِ الْفَحْشَاءِ وَالْمُنْكَرِ وَالْبَغْيِ يَعِظُكُمْ لَعَلَّكُمْ تَذَكَّرُونَ

Allāh commands justice, the doing of good, and liberality to kith and kin, and He forbids all shameful deeds, and injustice and rebellion: He instructs you, that ye may receive admonition. [Al-Qur'an, 016.090, An-Nahl (The Bee)]

2.5.6. No Burden can be Placed upon a Soul Greater than that He can Bear

لا يُكَلِّفُ اللَّهُ نَفْسًا إِلا وُسْعَهَا لَهَا مَا كَسَبَتْ وَعَلَيْهَا مَا اكْتَسَبَتْ رَبَّنَا لا تُؤَاخِذْنَا إِنْ نَسِينَا أَوْ أَخْطَأْنَا رَبَّنَا وَلا تَحْمِلْ عَلَيْنَا إِصْرًا كَمَا حَمَلْتَهُ عَلَى الَّذِينَ مِنْ قَبْلِنَا رَبَّنَا وَلا تُحَمِّلْنَا مَا لا طَاقَةَ لَنَا بِهِ وَاعْفُ عَنَّا وَاغْفِرْ لَنَا وَارْحَمْنَا أَنْتَ مَوْلانَا فَانْصُرْنَا عَلَى الْقَوْمِ الْكَافِرِينَ

On no soul doth Allāh Place a burden greater than it can bear. It gets every good that it earns, and it suffers every ill that it earns. (Pray:) "Our Lord! Condemn us not if we forget or fall into error; our Lord! Lay not on us a burden Like that which Thou didst lay on those before us; Our Lord! Lay not on us a burden greater than we have strength to bear. Blot out our sins, and grant us forgiveness. Have mercy on us. Thou art our Protector; Help us against those who stand against faith." [Al-Qur'an, 002.286 (Al-Baqara)]

2.5.7 Kindness and Forgiveness are Necessary

ثُمَّ كَانَ مِنَ الَّذِينَ آمَنُوا وَتَوَاصَوْا بِالصَّبْرِ وَتَوَاصَوْا بِالْمَرْحَمَةِ

Then will he be of those who believe, and enjoin patience, (constancy, and self-restraint), and enjoin deeds of **kindness** and compassion. [Al-Qur'an, 090.017, Al-Balad (The City, This Countryside)]

2.5.8 Equal Justice for All

يَا أَيُّهَا الَّذِينَ آمَنُوا كُتِبَ عَلَيْكُمُ الْقِصَاصُ فِي الْقَتْلَى الْحُرُّ بِالْحُرِّ وَالْعَبْدُ بِالْعَبْدِ وَالأُنْثَى بِالأُنْثَى فَمَنْ عُفِيَ لَهُ مِنْ أَخِيهِ شَيْءٌ فَاتِّبَاعٌ بِالْمَعْرُوفِ وَأَدَاءٌ إِلَيْهِ بِإِحْسَانٍ ذَلِكَ تَخْفِيفٌ مِنْ رَبِّكُمْ وَرَحْمَةٌ فَمَنِ اعْتَدَى بَعْدَ ذَلِكَ فَلَهُ عَذَابٌ أَلِيمٌ

O ye who believe! the law of equality is prescribed to you in cases of murder: the free for the free, the slave for the slave, the woman for the woman. But if any remission is made by the brother of the slain, then grant any reasonable demand, and compensate him with handsome gratitude, this is a concession and a Mercy from your Lord. After this whoever exceeds the limits shall be in grave penalty. [Al-Qur'an, 002.178 (Al-Baqara)]

2.5.9 Safeguard of life

مِنْ أَجْلِ ذَلِكَ كَتَبْنَا عَلَى بَنِي إِسْرَائِيلَ أَنَّهُ مَنْ قَتَلَ نَفْسًا بِغَيْرِ نَفْسٍ أَوْ فَسَادٍ فِي الأَرْضِ فَكَأَنَّمَا قَتَلَ النَّاسَ جَمِيعًا وَمَنْ أَحْيَاهَا فَكَأَنَّمَا أَحْيَا النَّاسَ جَمِيعًا وَلَقَدْ جَاءَتْهُمْ رُسُلُنَا بِالْبَيِّنَاتِ ثُمَّ إِنَّ كَثِيرًا مِنْهُمْ بَعْدَ ذَلِكَ فِي الأَرْضِ لَمُسْرِفُونَ

On that account: We ordained for the Children of Israel that if any one slew a person—unless it be for murder or for spreading mischief in the land—it would be as if he slew the whole people: and if any one saved a life, it would be as if he saved the life of the whole people. Then although there came to them Our messengers with clear signs, yet, even after that, many of them continued to commit excesses in the land. [Al-Qur'an, 005.032, Al-Maeda (The Table, The Table Spread)]

2.5.10. Exile from their Home is Punishable

ثُمَّ أَنْتُمْ هَؤُلاءِ تَقْتُلُونَ أَنْفُسَكُمْ وَتُخْرِجُونَ فَرِيقًا مِنْكُمْ مِنْ دِيَارِهِمْ تَظَاهَرُونَ عَلَيْهِمْ بِالإِثْمِ وَالْعُدْوَانِ وَإِنْ يَأْتُوكُمْ أُسَارَى تُفَادُوهُمْ وَهُوَ مُحَرَّمٌ عَلَيْكُمْ إِخْرَاجُهُمْ أَفَتُؤْمِنُونَ بِبَعْضِ الْكِتَابِ وَتَكْفُرُونَ بِبَعْضٍ فَمَا جَزَاءُ مَنْ يَفْعَلُ ذَلِكَ مِنْكُمْ إِلا خِزْيٌ فِي الْحَيَاةِ الدُّنْيَا وَيَوْمَ الْقِيَامَةِ يُرَدُّونَ إِلَى أَشَدِّ الْعَذَابِ وَمَا اللَّهُ بِغَافِلٍ عَمَّا تَعْمَلُونَ

After this it is ye, the same people, who slay among yourselves, and banish a party of you from their homes; assist (Their enemies) against them, in guilt and rancour; and if they come to you as captives, ye ransom them, though it was not lawful for you to banish them. Then is it only a part of the Book that ye believe in, and do ye reject the rest? but what is the reward for those among you who behave like this but disgrace in this life?—and on the Day of Judgment they shall be consigned to the most grievous penalty. For Allāh is not unmindful of what ye do. [Al-Qur'an, 002.08, Al-Baqara (The Cow)]

2.5.11. Protection of Chastity

الزَّانِيَةُ وَالزَّانِي فَاجْلِدُوا كُلَّ وَاحِدٍ مِنْهُمَا مِائَةَ جَلْدَةٍ وَلا تَأْخُذْكُمْ بِهِمَا رَأْفَةٌ فِي دِينِ اللَّهِ إِنْ كُنْتُمْ تُؤْمِنُونَ بِاللَّهِ وَالْيَوْمِ الآخِرِ وَلْيَشْهَدْ عَذَابَهُمَا طَائِفَةٌ مِنَ الْمُؤْمِنِينَ

The woman and the man guilty of adultery or fornication,—flog each of them with a hundred stripes: Let not compassion move you in their case, in a matter prescribed by Allāh, if ye believe in Allāh and the Last Day: and let a party of the Believers witness their punishment. [Al-Qur'an, 024.00, An-Noor (The Light)]

يَا أَيُّهَا النَّبِيُّ قُلْ لأَزْوَاجِكَ وَبَنَاتِكَ وَنِسَاءِ الْمُؤْمِنِينَ يُدْنِينَ عَلَيْهِنَّ مِنْ جَلابِيبِهِنَّ ذَلِكَ أَدْنَى أَنْ يُعْرَفْنَ فَلا يُؤْذَيْنَ وَكَانَ اللَّهُ غَفُورًا رَحِيمًا

O Prophet! Tell thy wives and daughters, and the believing women, that they should cast their outer garments over their persons (when abroad): that is most convenient, that they should be known (as such) and not molested. And Allāh is Oft-Forgiving, Most Merciful. [Al-Qur'an, 033.059, Al-Ahzab (The Clans, the Coalition, the Combined Forces)]

2.5.12 Praise God for Beautiful (Gifts)

قُلْ مَنْ حَرَّمَ زِينَةَ اللَّهِ الَّتِي أَخْرَجَ لِعِبَادِهِ وَالطَّيِّبَاتِ مِنَ الرِّزْقِ قُلْ هِيَ لِلَّذِينَ آمَنُوا فِي الْحَيَاةِ الدُّنْيَا خَالِصَةً يَوْمَ الْقِيَامَةِ كَذَٰلِكَ نُفَصِّلُ الْآيَاتِ لِقَوْمٍ يَعْلَمُونَ

Say: Who hath forbidden the beautiful (gifts) of Allāh, which He hath produced for His servants, and the things, clean and pure, (which He hath provided) for sustenance? Say: They are, in the life of this world, for those who believe, (and) purely for them on the Day of Judgement. Thus, do We explain the signs in detail for those who understand. [Al-Qur'an, 007.03, Al-Araf (The Heights)]

2.5.13. Freedom to Chose Spouse

وَإِنْ خِفْتُمْ أَلَّا تُقْسِطُوا فِي الْيَتَامَىٰ فَانْكِحُوا مَا طَابَ لَكُمْ مِنَ النِّسَاءِ مَثْنَىٰ وَثُلَاثَ وَرُبَاعَ فَإِنْ خِفْتُمْ أَلَّا تَعْدِلُوا فَوَاحِدَةً أَوْ مَا مَلَكَتْ أَيْمَانُكُمْ ذَٰلِكَ أَدْنَىٰ أَلَّا تَعُولُوا

If ye fear that ye shall not be able to deal justly with the orphans, Marry women of your choice, Two or three or four; but if ye fear that ye shall not be able to deal justly (with them), then only one, or (a captive) that your right hands possess, that will be more suitable, to prevent you from doing injustice. [Al-Qur'an, 004.00, An-Nisa (Women)]

يَا أَيُّهَا الَّذِينَ آمَنُوا لَا يَحِلُّ لَكُمْ أَنْ تَرِثُوا النِّسَاءَ كَرْهًا وَلَا تَعْضُلُوهُنَّ لِتَذْهَبُوا بِبَعْضِ مَا آتَيْتُمُوهُنَّ إِلَّا أَنْ يَأْتِينَ بِفَاحِشَةٍ مُبَيِّنَةٍ وَعَاشِرُوهُنَّ بِالْمَعْرُوفِ فَإِنْ كَرِهْتُمُوهُنَّ فَعَسَىٰ أَنْ تَكْرَهُوا شَيْئًا وَيَجْعَلَ اللَّهُ فِيهِ خَيْرًا كَثِيرًا

O ye who believe! Ye are forbidden to inherit women

against their will. Nor should ye treat them with harshness, that ye may Take away part of the dower ye have given them,-except where they have been guilty of open lewdness; on the contrary live with them on a footing of kindness and equity. If ye take a dislike to them it may be that ye dislike a thing, and Allāh brings about through it a great deal of good. (Al-Qur'an, 004.01, An-Nisa (Women)]

2.5.14. No Boundation of Religion

لا إِكْرَاهَ فِي الدِّينِ قَدْ تَبَيَّنَ الرُّشْدُ مِنَ الْغَيِّ فَمَنْ يَكْفُرْ بِالطَّاغُوتِ وَيُؤْمِنْ بِاللَّهِ فَقَدِ اسْتَمْسَكَ بِالْعُرْوَةِ الْوُثْقَى لا انْفِصَامَ لَهَا وَاللَّهُ سَمِيعٌ عَلِيمٌ

Let there be **no compulsion in religion**: Truth stands out clear from Error: whoever rejects evil and believes in Allāh hath grasped the most trustworthy hand-hold that never breaks. And Allāh heareth and knoweth all things. [Al-Qur'an, 002.25, (Al-Baqara)]

وَلَوْ شَاءَ رَبُّكَ لآمَنَ مَنْ فِي الأَرْضِ كُلُّهُمْ جَمِيعًا أَفَأَنْتَ تُكْرِهُ النَّاسَ حَتَّى يَكُونُوا مُؤْمِنِينَ

If it had been thy Lord's will, they would all have believed, all who are on earth! wilt thou then compel mankind, against their will, to believe! [Al-Qur'an, 010.09, Yunus (Jonah)]

2.5.15 Evil not to be Noised Publically

لا يُحِبُّ اللَّهُ الْجَهْرَ بِالسُّوءِ مِنَ الْقَوْلِ إِلا مَنْ ظُلِمَ وَكَانَ اللَّهُ سَمِيعًا عَلِيمًا

Allāh loveth not that evil should be noised abroad in public speech, except where injustice hath been done; for Allāh is He who heareth and knoweth all things. [Al-Qur'an, 004.14, An-Nisa (Women)]

2.5.16. Protection against Malevolent Scandle and Libel [Al-Qur'an, 004.14, An-Nisa (Women)]

2.5.17. Proof is Necessary Considered Innocent

لَوْلا إِذْ سَمِعْتُمُوهُ ظَنَّ الْمُؤْمِنُونَ وَالْمُؤْمِنَاتُ بِأَنْفُسِهِمْ خَيْرًا وَقَالُوا هَذَا إِفْكٌ مُبِينٌ

Why did not the believers—men and women—when ye heard of the affair,—put the best construction on it in their own minds and say, "This (charge) is an obvious lie"? [Al-Qur'an, 024.012 (An-Noor)]

لَوْلا جَاءُوا عَلَيْهِ بِأَرْبَعَةِ شُهَدَاءَ فَإِذْ لَمْ يَأْتُوا بِالشُّهَدَاءِ فَأُولَئِكَ عِنْدَ اللَّهِ هُمُ الْكَاذِبُونَ

Why did they not bring four witnesses to prove it? When they have not brought the witnesses, such men, in the sight of Allāh, (stand forth) themselves as liars! [Al-Qur'an, 024.013 (An-Noor)]

2.5.18. Nobody can be Stopped from the Path of Allāh

قُلْ يَا أَهْلَ الْكِتَابِ لِمَ تَصُدُّونَ عَنْ سَبِيلِ اللَّهِ مَنْ آمَنَ تَبْغُونَهَا عِوَجًا وَأَنْتُمْ شُهَدَاءُ وَمَا اللَّهُ بِغَافِلٍ عَمَّا تَعْمَلُونَ

Say: "O ye People of the Book! Why obstruct ye those who believe, from the path of Allāh, Seeking to make it crooked, while ye were yourselves witnesses (to Allāh's Covenant)? but Allāh is not unmindful of all that ye do." [Al-Qur'an, 003.09, Aal-E-Imran (The Family of Imran)]

2.5.19. One Should Fulfil Promises and Justice in Measurement

وَلا تَقْرَبُوا مَالَ الْيَتِيمِ إِلا بِالَّتِي هِيَ أَحْسَنُ حَتَّى يَبْلُغَ أَشُدَّهُ وَأَوْفُوا الْكَيْلَ وَالْمِيزَانَ بِالْقِسْطِ لا نُكَلِّفُ نَفْسًا إِلا وُسْعَهَا وَإِذَا قُلْتُمْ فَاعْدِلُوا وَلَوْ كَانَ ذَا قُرْبَى وَبِعَهْدِ اللَّهِ أَوْفُوا ذَلِكُمْ وَصَّاكُمْ بِهِ لَعَلَّكُمْ تَذَكَّرُونَ

And come not nigh to the orphan's property, except to improve it, until he attain the age of full strength; give measure and weight with (full) justice;—no burden do We place on any soul, but that which it can bear;—whenever ye speak, speak justly, even if a near relative is concerned; and fulfil the covenant of Allāh: thus doth He command you, that ye may remember. [Al-Qur'an, 006.15, Al-Anaam (Cattle, Livestock)]

وَأَوْفُوا الْكَيْلَ إِذَا كِلْتُمْ وَزِنُوا بِالْقِسْطَاسِ الْمُسْتَقِيمِ ذَلِكَ خَيْرٌ وَأَحْسَنُ تَأْوِيلا

Give full measure when ye measure, and weigh with a balance that is straight: that is the most fitting and the most advantageous in the final determination. [Al-Qur'an, 017.03, Al-Isra (Isra, The Night Journey, Children of Israel)]

2.5.20. Allāh's Bounties must not be Closed Upon anyone

كُلا نُمِدُّ هَؤُلاءِ وَهَؤُلاءِ مِنْ عَطَاءِ رَبِّكَ وَمَا كَانَ عَطَاءُ رَبِّكَ مَحْظُورًا

Of the bounties of thy Lord We bestow freely on all—These as well as those: The bounties of thy Lord are not closed (to anyone). [Al-Qur'an, 017.020 (Al-Isra)]

2.5.21. Proof of Allāh

وَمِنْ آيَاتِهِ خَلْقُ السَّمَاوَاتِ وَالأَرْضِ وَاخْتِلافُ أَلْسِنَتِكُمْ وَأَلْوَانِكُمْ إِنَّ فِي ذَلِكَ لآيَاتٍ لِلْعَالِمِينَ

And among His Signs is the creation of the heavens and the earth, and the variations in your languages and your colours: verily in that are Signs for those who know. [Al-Qur'an, 030.02, Ar-Room (The Romans, The Byzantines)]

2.5.22. Knowledge (3 to 5:96 and speech (4:55)

اقْرَأْ وَرَبُّكَ الأَكْرَمُ

Proclaim! And thy Lord is Most Bountiful. [Al-Qur'an, 096.00, Al-Alaq (The Clot, Read)]

الَّذِي عَلَّمَ بِالْقَلَمِ

He Who taught (the use of) the pen. [Al-Qur'an, 096.004 (Al-Alaq)]

عَلَّمَ الإِنْسَانَ مَا لَمْ يَعْلَمْ

Taught man that which he knew not. [Al-Qur'an, 096.005 (Al-Alaq)]

عَلَّمَهُ الْبَيَانَ

He has taught him speech (and intelligence). [Al-Qur'an, 055.00, Ar-Rahman (The Beneficent, The Mercy Giving)]

The Holy Qur'an is, indeed, a wonderful book: it is exactly what a book of right guidance ought to be. It throws light on complex problems of the Universe on the one hand, and gives guidance in respect of very important problems of human life on the other. It gives us the permanent values of life, which form the very foundation ofeducation and culture, as well as directions about the everyday civic life of a man.

2.6 Norms of Good Character

A man's social and civic life starts from everyday thinker, but, infact these common relationships are the foundations on which big civilizations are not only buily but with the members of our family, with friends, with neighbours, with relatives, with common acquaintances, with foreigners, also what our mode of living, walking about eating and drinking, talking with each other and in gatherings etc, should be. National Character is reflected from these common behaviours; therefore, the Holy Qur'an emphasises goodness, beauty and virtue in these aspectis of life also. For example—

2.6.1 Manners of Meeting Each Other

When a (courteous) greeting is offered to you, meet it with a greeting still more courteous, or (at least) of equal courtesy. Do it when even if you enter Your own houses. or you enter others houses or even if an ignorant man addresses you. All believers are brother to each other.

وَإِذَا حُيِّيتُمْ بِتَحِيَّةٍ فَحَيُّوا بِأَحْسَنَ مِنْهَا أَوْ رُدُّوهَا إِنَّ اللَّهَ كَانَ عَلَى كُلِّ شَيْءٍ حَسِيبًا

[Al-Qur'an, 004.08, An-Nisa (Women)]

لَيْسَ عَلَى الأَعْمَى حَرَجٌ وَلا عَلَى الأَعْرَجِ حَرَجٌ وَلا عَلَى الْمَرِيضِ حَرَجٌ وَلا عَلَى أَنْفُسِكُمْ أَنْ تَأْكُلُوا مِنْ بُيُوتِكُمْ أَوْ بُيُوتِ آبَائِكُمْ أَوْ بُيُوتِ أُمَّهَاتِكُمْ أَوْ بُيُوتِ إِخْوَانِكُمْ أَوْ بُيُوتِ أَخَوَاتِكُمْ أَوْ بُيُوتِ أَعْمَامِكُمْ أَوْ بُيُوتِ عَمَّاتِكُمْ أَوْ بُيُوتِ أَخْوَالِكُمْ أَوْ بُيُوتِ خَالاتِكُمْ أَوْ مَا مَلَكْتُمْ مَفَاتِحَهُ أَوْ صَدِيقِكُمْ لَيْسَ عَلَيْكُمْ جُنَاحٌ أَنْ تَأْكُلُوا جَمِيعًا أَوْ أَشْتَاتًا فَإِذَا دَخَلْتُمْ بُيُوتًا فَسَلِّمُوا عَلَى أَنْفُسِكُمْ تَحِيَّةً مِنْ عِنْدِ اللَّهِ مُبَارَكَةً طَيِّبَةً كَذَلِكَ يُبَيِّنُ اللَّهُ لَكُمُ الآيَاتِ لَعَلَّكُمْ تَعْقِلُونَ

It is no fault in the blind nor in one born lame, nor in one afflicted with illness, nor in yourselves, that ye should eat in your own houses, or those of your fathers, or your mothers, or your brothers, or your sisters, or your father's brothers or your father's sisters, or your mother's brothers, or your mother's sisters, or in houses of which the keys are in your possession, or in the house of a sincere friend of yours: there is no blame on you, whether ye eat in company or separately. But if ye enter houses, **salute each other**—a greeting of blessing and purity as from Allāh. Thus does Allāh make clear the signs to you: that ye may understand. [Al-Qur'an, 024.06, An-Noor (The Light)]

إِنَّمَا الْمُؤْمِنُونَ إِخْوَةٌ فَأَصْلِحُوا بَيْنَ أَخَوَيْكُمْ وَاتَّقُوا اللَّهَ لَعَلَّكُمْ تُرْحَمُونَ

The Believers are but a single Brotherhood: So, make peace and reconciliation between your two (contending) brothers; and fear Allāh, that ye may receive Mercy. [Al-Qur'an, 049.01, Al-Hujraat (The Private Apartments, The Inner Apartments)]

2.6.2 Manners of Conversation

Always say what is directed to the Right (in a straightforward manner, avoiding all circumlocutions). Speak in a language which is generally recognized as noble. Say those things that are best, Speak fair to the people. Lower your voice. Whenever you speak, speak justly, even if a near relative is concerned. Shun the word that is false. Cover not Truth with falsehood, nor conceal the Truth when you know what it is.

يَا أَيُّهَا الَّذِينَ آمَنُوا اتَّقُوا اللَّهَ وَقُولُوا قَوْلًا سَدِيدًا

O ye who believe! Fear Allāh, and (always) say a word directed to the Right: (Al-Qur'an, 033.07, Al-Ahzab (The Clans, the Coalition, the Combined Forces)]

وَقُلْ لِعِبَادِي يَقُولُوا الَّتِي هِيَ أَحْسَنُ إِنَّ الشَّيْطَانَ يَنْزَغُ بَيْنَهُمْ إِنَّ الشَّيْطَانَ كَانَ لِلْإِنْسَانِ عَدُوًّا مُبِينًا

Say to My servants that they should (only) say those things that are best: for Satan doth sow dissensions among them: For Satan is to man an avowed enemy. [Al-Qur'an, 017.053 (Al-Isra)

وَاقْصِدْ فِي مَشْيِكَ وَاغْضُضْ مِنْ صَوْتِكَ إِنَّ أَنْكَرَ الْأَصْوَاتِ لَصَوْتُ الْحَمِيرِ

"And be moderate in thy pace, and lower thy voice; for the harshest of sounds without doubt is the braying of the ass." (Al-Qur'an, 031.01, Luqman (Luqman)]

وَلَا تَقْرَبُوا مَالَ الْيَتِيمِ إِلَّا بِالَّتِي هِيَ أَحْسَنُ حَتَّى يَبْلُغَ أَشُدَّهُ وَأَوْفُوا الْكَيْلَ وَالْمِيزَانَ بِالْقِسْطِ لَا نُكَلِّفُ نَفْسًا إِلَّا وُسْعَهَا وَإِذَا قُلْتُمْ فَاعْدِلُوا وَلَوْ كَانَ ذَا قُرْبَى وَبِعَهْدِ اللَّهِ أَوْفُوا ذَلِكُمْ وَصَّاكُمْ بِهِ لَعَلَّكُمْ تَذَكَّرُونَ

And come not nigh to the orphan's property, except to improve it, until he attain the age of full strength; give measure and weight with (full) justice;- no burden do We place on any soul, but that which it can bear;- whenever ye speak, speak justly, even if a near relative is concerned; and fulfil the covenant of Allāh: thus doth He command you, that ye may remember. (Al-Qur'an, 006.15, Al-Anaam (Cattle, Livestock)]

وَلَا تَلْبِسُوا الْحَقَّ بِالْبَاطِلِ وَتَكْتُمُوا الْحَقَّ وَأَنْتُمْ تَعْلَمُونَ

And cover not Truth with falsehood, nor conceal the Truth when ye know (what it is). (Al-Qur'an, 002.04, Al-Baqara (The Cow)]

2.6.3 Avoid Vain Talks and Deeds

Come not near shameful deeds, whether open or secret. Avoid vain talk. Do not listen to vain talk. Witness no falsehood. If you have to pass by futility, pass by it with honourable avoidance. In the life of eternal peace no vain discources will be heard. Avoid shameful deeds. Broadcast no scandals.

قُلْ تَعَالَوْا أَتْلُ مَا حَرَّمَ رَبُّكُمْ عَلَيْكُمْ أَلاَّ تُشْرِكُوا بِهِ شَيْئًا وَبِالْوَالِدَيْنِ إِحْسَانًا وَلاَ تَقْتُلُوا أَوْلاَدَكُمْ مِنْ إِمْلاَقٍ نَحْنُ نَرْزُقُكُمْ وَإِيَّاهُمْ وَلاَ تَقْرَبُوا الْفَوَاحِشَ مَا ظَهَرَ مِنْهَا وَمَا بَطَنَ وَلاَ تَقْتُلُوا النَّفْسَ الَّتِي حَرَّمَ اللَّهُ إِلاَّ بِالْحَقِّ ذَلِكُمْ وَصَّاكُمْ بِهِ لَعَلَّكُمْ تَعْقِلُونَ

"Come, I will rehearse what Allāh hath (really) prohibited you from": Join not anything as equal with Him; be good to your parents; kill not your children on a plea of want;- We provide sustenance for you and for them;- come not nigh to shameful deeds. Whether open or secret; take not life, which Allāh hath made sacred, except by way of justice and law: thus doth He command you, that ye may learn wisdom. (Al-Qur'an, 006.15, Al-Anaam (Cattle, Livestock)]

وَالَّذِينَ هُمْ عَنِ اللَّغْوِ مُعْرِضُونَ

Who avoid vain talk. [Al-Qur'an, 023.00, Al-Mumenoon (The Believers)]

وَالَّذِينَ لاَ يَشْهَدُونَ الزُّورَ وَإِذَا مَرُّوا بِاللَّغْوِ مَرُّوا كِرَامًا

Those who witness no falsehood, and, if they pass by futility, they pass by it with honourable (avoidance). (Al-Qur'an, 025.07, Al-Furqan (The Criterion, The Standard)]

لاَ يَسْمَعُونَ فِيهَا لَغْوًا إِلاَّ سَلاَمًا وَلَهُمْ رِزْقُهُمْ فِيهَا بُكْرَةً وَعَشِيًّا

They will not there hear any vain discourse, but only salutations of Peace: And they will have therein their sustenance, morning and evening. [Al-Qur'an, 019.06, Maryam (Mary)]

لا يَسْمَعُونَ فِيهَا لَغْوًا وَلا كِذَّابًا

No vanity shall they hear therein, nor Untruth. (Al-Qur'an, 078.03, an-Naba (The Tidings, The Announcement)]

قُلْ إِنَّمَا حَرَّمَ رَبِّيَ الْفَوَاحِشَ مَا ظَهَرَ مِنْهَا وَمَا بَطَنَ وَالإِثْمَ وَالْبَغْيَ بِغَيْرِ الْحَقِّ وَأَنْ تُشْرِكُوا بِاللَّهِ مَا لَمْ يُنَزِّلْ بِهِ سُلْطَانًا وَأَنْ تَقُولُوا عَلَى اللَّهِ مَا لا تَعْلَمُونَ

Say: the things that my Lord hath indeed forbidden are: shameful deeds, whether open or secret; sins and trespasses against truth or reason; assigning of partners to Allāh, for which He hath given no authority; and saying things about Allāh of which ye have no knowledge. [Al-Qur'an, 007.03, Al-Araf (The Heights)]

إِنَّ الَّذِينَ يُحِبُّونَ أَنْ تَشِيعَ الْفَاحِشَةُ فِي الَّذِينَ آمَنُوا لَهُمْ عَذَابٌ أَلِيمٌ فِي الدُّنْيَا وَالآخِرَةِ وَاللَّهُ يَعْلَمُ وَأَنْتُمْ لا تَعْلَمُونَ

Those who love (to see) scandal published broadcast among the Believers, will have a grievous Penalty in this life and in the Hereafter: Allāh knows, and ye know not. (Al-Qur'an, 024.01, An-Noor (The Light)]

2.6.4 Manners of Walking

Walk not on the earth with insolence, for you cannot rend the earth asunder, not reach the mountains in height. Swell not your cheeks (for pride) at men, not walk in insolence through the earth for Allāh loves not the arrogant boaster. Beware of the tricks that deceive with the eyes and that hearts conceal. Walk on the earth in humility. Women should walk bashfully (25:28). Women should not display their beauty and ornaments except what most ordinarily appears thereof; they should draw their veils over their bosoms and not display their beauty........ they should not strike their feet in order to draw attention of their hidden ornaments. Man and women both should lower their gaze and guard their modesty. Beware of the tricks that deceive with the eyes and that hearts conceal

وَلا تَمْشِ فِي الأَرْضِ مَرَحًا إِنَّكَ لَنْ تَخْرِقَ الأَرْضَ وَلَنْ تَبْلُغَ الجِبَالَ طُولا

Nor walk on the earth with insolence: for thou canst not rend the earth asunder, nor reach the mountains in height. [Al-Qur'an, 017.037 (Al-Isra)]

وَلا تُصَعِّرْ خَدَّكَ لِلنَّاسِ وَلا تَمْشِ فِي الأَرْضِ مَرَحًا إِنَّ اللهَ لا يُحِبُّ كُلَّ مُخْتَالٍ فَخُورٍ.

"And swell not thy cheek (for pride) at men, nor walk in insolence through the earth; for Allāh loveth not any arrogant boaster. [Al-Qur'an, 031.01, Luqman (Luqman)]

وَعِبَادُ الرَّحْمَنِ الَّذِينَ يَمْشُونَ عَلَى الأَرْضِ هَوْنًا وَإِذَا خَاطَبَهُمُ الجَاهِلُونَ قَالُوا سَلامًا

And the servants of (Allāh) Most Gracious are those who walk on the earth in humility, and when the ignorant address them, they say, "Peace!". [Al-Qur'an, 025.06, Al-Furqan (The Criterion, The Standard)]

2.6.5. Avoid Suspicion Without Verifying

Pursue not that of which you have no knowledge. Avoid suspicion as far as possible and spy not on each other, not speak ill of each other behind their backs. It is like eating flesh of one's brother. Think of everybody as innocent till guilt is proved against him. If a wicked person comes to you with any news, ascertain the truth. Refer matters that touch pubic safety or fear to men charged with authority for proper investigation. Evil must not be noised abroad in public speech except where injustice where injustice has been done.

وَلا تَقْفُ مَا لَيْسَ لَكَ بِهِ عِلْمٌ إِنَّ السَّمْعَ وَالْبَصَرَ وَالْفُؤَادَ كُلُّ أُولَئِكَ كَانَ عَنْهُ مَسْئُولا

And pursue not that of which thou hast no knowledge; for every act of hearing, or of seeing or of (feeling in) the heart will be enquired into (on the Day of Reckoning). [Al-Qur'an, 017.036 (Al-Isra)]

يَا أَيُّهَا الَّذِينَ آمَنُوا اجْتَنِبُوا كَثِيرًا مِنَ الظَّنِّ إِنَّ بَعْضَ الظَّنِّ إِثْمٌ وَلا تَجَسَّسُوا وَلا يَغْتَبْ بَعْضُكُمْ بَعْضًا أَيُحِبُّ أَحَدُكُمْ أَنْ يَأْكُلَ لَحْمَ أَخِيهِ مَيْتًا فَكَرِهْتُمُوهُ وَاتَّقُوا اللَّهَ إِنَّ اللَّهَ تَوَّابٌ رَحِيمٌ

O ye who believe! Avoid suspicion as much (as possible): for suspicion in some cases is a sin: And spy not on each other behind their backs. Would any of you like to eat the flesh of his dead brother? Nay, ye would abhor it...But fear Allāh: For Allāh is Oft-Returning, Most Merciful. [Al-Qur'an, 049.01, Al-Hujraat)

يَا أَيُّهَا الَّذِينَ آمَنُوا إِنْ جَاءَكُمْ فَاسِقٌ بِنَبَإٍ فَتَبَيَّنُوا أَنْ تُصِيبُوا قَوْمًا بِجَهَالَةٍ فَتُصْبِحُوا عَلَى مَا فَعَلْتُمْ نَادِمِينَ

O ye who believe! If a wicked person comes to you with any news, ascertain the truth, lest ye harm people unwittingly and afterwards become full of repentance for what ye have done. [Al-Qur'an, 049.006 (Al-Hujraat)]

وَإِذَا جَاءَهُمْ أَمْرٌ مِنَ الأَمْنِ أَوِ الْخَوْفِ أَذَاعُوا بِهِ وَلَوْ رَدُّوهُ إِلَى الرَّسُولِ وَإِلَى أُولِي الأَمْرِ مِنْهُمْ لَعَلِمَهُ الَّذِينَ يَسْتَنْبِطُونَهُ مِنْهُمْ وَلَوْلا فَضْلُ اللهِ عَلَيْكُمْ وَرَحْمَتُهُ لاتَّبَعْتُمُ الشَّيْطَانَ إِلا قَلِيلا

Allāh loveth not that evil should be noised abroad in public speech, except where injustice hath been done; for Allāh is He who heareth and knoweth all things. [Al-Qur'an, 004.08, An-Nisa (Women)]

2.6.6 Do not Abuse Innocent and Chaste Persons

Slander not chaste women. Those who slander chaste women, indiscreet but believing, are cursed in this life and in the Hereafter: for them is a grievous Penalty. If anyone earns a sin or a fault and throws it on to one who is innocent, he carries on himself both a falsehood and flagrant sin.)

وَالَّذِينَ يَرْمُونَ الْمُحْصَنَاتِ ثُمَّ لَمْ يَأْتُوا بِأَرْبَعَةِ شُهَدَاءَ فَاجْلِدُوهُمْ ثَمَانِينَ جَلْدَةً وَلَا تَقْبَلُوا لَهُمْ شَهَادَةً أَبَدًا وَأُولَئِكَ هُمُ الْفَاسِقُونَ

And those who launch a charge against chaste women, and produce not four witnesses (to support their allegations),—flog them with eighty stripes; and reject their evidence ever after: for such men are wicked transgressors. [Al-Qur'an, 024.00, An-Noor (The Light)]

وَمَنْ يَكْسِبْ خَطِيئَةً أَوْ إِثْمًا ثُمَّ يَرْمِ بِهِ بَرِيئًا فَقَدِ احْتَمَلَ بُهْتَانًا وَإِثْمًا مُبِينًا

But if any one earns a fault or a sin and throws it on to one that is innocent, He carries (on himself) (Both) a falsehood and a flagrant sin. [Al-Qur'an, 004.11, An-Nisa (Women)]

2.6.7 Molestation Strictly Prohibited

يَا أَيُّهَا النَّبِيُّ قُلْ لِأَزْوَاجِكَ وَبَنَاتِكَ وَنِسَاءِ الْمُؤْمِنِينَ يُدْنِينَ عَلَيْهِنَّ مِنْ جَلَابِيبِهِنَّ ذَلِكَ أَدْنَى أَنْ يُعْرَفْنَ فَلَا يُؤْذَيْنَ وَكَانَ اللَّهُ غَفُورًا رَحِيمًا

O Prophet! Tell thy wives and daughters, and the believing women, that they should cast their outer garments over their persons (when abroad): that is most convenient, that they should be known (as such) and not molested. And Allāh is Oft-Forgiving, Most Merciful. [Al-Qur'an, 033.059]

2.6.8 Back-biting, Allegation, Jealousy etc.

Speak not ill of each other backs. Let no men and women laugh at others. Those who slander such of the believers as give themselves freely to (deeds of) charity, as well as such as can find nothing to give except the fruits of their labour, and throw ridicule on them, Allāh will throw back their ridicule on them: and they shall have a grievous penalty. Leave alone those who take their religion to be mere play and amusement and are deceived by the life of this world. Donot defame or be sarcastic to each other. Call not each other by offensive nicknames. Envy not mankind for what Allāh has given them of His bounty.

يَا أَيُّهَا الَّذِينَ آمَنُوا اجْتَنِبُوا كَثِيرًا مِنَ الظَّنِّ إِنَّ بَعْضَ الظَّنِّ إِثْمٌ وَلَا تَجَسَّسُوا وَلَا يَغْتَبْ بَعْضُكُمْ بَعْضًا أَيُحِبُّ أَحَدُكُمْ أَنْ يَأْكُلَ لَحْمَ أَخِيهِ مَيْتًا فَكَرِهْتُمُوهُ وَاتَّقُوا اللَّهَ إِنَّ اللَّهَ تَوَّابٌ رَحِيمٌ

O ye who believe! Avoid suspicion as much (as possible): for suspicion in some cases is a sin: And spy not on each other behind their backs. Would any of you like to eat the flesh of his dead brother? Nay, ye would abhor it...But fear Allāh: For Allāh is Oft-Returning, Most Merciful. [Al-Qur'an, 049.012 (Al-Hujraat)]

يَا أَيُّهَا الَّذِينَ آمَنُوا لَا يَسْخَرْ قَوْمٌ مِنْ قَوْمٍ عَسَى أَنْ يَكُونُوا خَيْرًا مِنْهُمْ وَلَا نِسَاءٌ مِنْ نِسَاءٍ عَسَى أَنْ يَكُنَّ خَيْرًا مِنْهُنَّ وَلَا تَلْمِزُوا أَنْفُسَكُمْ وَلَا تَنَابَزُوا بِالْأَلْقَابِ بِئْسَ الاسْمُ الْفُسُوقُ بَعْدَ الْإِيمَانِ وَمَنْ لَمْ يَتُبْ فَأُولَئِكَ هُمُ الظَّالِمُونَ

O ye who believe! Let not some men among you laugh at others: It may be that the (latter) are better than the (former): Nor let some women laugh at others: It may be that the (latter are better than the (former): Nor defame nor be sarcastic to each other, nor call each other by (offensive) nicknames: Ill-seeming is a name connoting wickedness, (to be used of one) after he has believed: And those who do not desist are (indeed) doing wrong. [Al-Qur'an, 049.01, Al-Hujraat (The Private Apartments, The Inner Apartments)]

الَّذِينَ يَلْمِزُونَ الْمُطَّوِّعِينَ مِنَ الْمُؤْمِنِينَ فِي الصَّدَقَاتِ وَالَّذِينَ لَا يَجِدُونَ إِلَّا جُهْدَهُمْ فَيَسْخَرُونَ مِنْهُمْ سَخِرَ اللَّهُ مِنْهُمْ وَلَهُمْ عَذَابٌ أَلِيمٌ

Those who slander such of the believers as give themselves

freely to (deeds of) charity, as well as such as can find nothing to give except the fruits of their labour,—and throw ridicule on them,—Allāh will throw back their ridicule on them: and they shall have a grievous penalty. (Al-Qur'an, 009.07, At-Tawba (Repentance, Dispensation)]

2.6.9 Manners to Enter Other's House and Feast

Enter not any one's house without permission. If you find no one in the house, enter not unless permission is given to you. If you are asked to go back, go back. No fault, if you enter houses not used for living and which serve some (other) use for you. When called to decide on a matter required collective action, do not depart without permission. When invited to a meal do not go early to wait for its preparation, but enter when you are invited. And when you haven taken your meal, disperse, without seeking familiar talk. When you ask for anything you want, ask them from before a screen.

يَا أَيُّهَا الَّذِينَ آمَنُوا لا تَدْخُلُوا بُيُوتًا غَيْرَ بُيُوتِكُمْ حَتَّى تَسْتَأْنِسُوا وَتُسَلِّمُوا عَلَى أَهْلِهَا ذَلِكُمْ خَيْرٌ لَكُمْ لَعَلَّكُمْ تَذَكَّرُونَ

O ye who believe! enter not houses other than your own, until ye have asked permission and saluted those in them: that is best for you, in order that ye may heed (what is seemly). [Al-Qur'an, 024.027]

فَإِنْ لَمْ تَجِدُوا فِيهَا أَحَدًا فَلا تَدْخُلُوهَا حَتَّى يُؤْذَنَ لَكُمْ وَإِنْ قِيلَ لَكُمُ ارْجِعُوا فَارْجِعُوا هُوَ أَزْكَى لَكُمْ وَاللَّهُ بِمَا تَعْمَلُونَ عَلِيمٌ

If ye find no one in the house, enter not until permission is given to you: if ye are asked to go back, go back: that makes for greater purity for yourselves: and Allāh knows well all that ye do. (Al-Qur'an, 024.028)

لَيْسَ عَلَيْكُمْ جُنَاحٌ أَنْ تَدْخُلُوا بُيُوتًا غَيْرَ مَسْكُونَةٍ فِيهَا مَتَاعٌ لَكُمْ وَاللَّهُ يَعْلَمُ مَا تُبْدُونَ وَمَا تَكْتُمُونَ

It is no fault on your part to enter houses not used for living in, which serve some (other) use for you: And Allāh has knowledge of what ye reveal and what ye conceal.

(Al-Qur'an, 024.029 (An-Noor)

يَا أَيُّهَا الَّذِينَ آمَنُوا لا تَدْخُلُوا بُيُوتَ النَّبِيِّ إِلا أَنْ يُؤْذَنَ لَكُمْ إِلَى طَعَامٍ غَيْرَ نَاظِرِينَ إِنَاهُ وَلَكِنْ إِذَا دُعِيتُمْ فَادْخُلُوا فَإِذَا طَعِمْتُمْ فَانْتَشِرُوا وَلا مُسْتَأْنِسِينَ لِحَدِيثٍ إِنَّ ذَلِكُمْ كَانَ يُؤْذِي النَّبِيَّ فَيَسْتَحْيِي مِنْكُمْ وَاللَّهُ لا يَسْتَحْيِي مِنَ الْحَقِّ وَإِذَا سَأَلْتُمُوهُنَّ مَتَاعًا فَاسْأَلُوهُنَّ مِنْ وَرَاءِ حِجَابٍ ذَلِكُمْ أَطْهَرُ لِقُلُوبِكُمْ وَقُلُوبِهِنَّ وَمَا كَانَ لَكُمْ أَنْ تُؤْذُوا رَسُولَ اللَّهِ وَلا أَنْ تَنْكِحُوا أَزْوَاجَهُ مِنْ بَعْدِهِ أَبَدًا إِنَّ ذَلِكُمْ كَانَ عِنْدَ اللَّهِ عَظِيمًا

O ye who believe! Enter not the Prophet's houses,—until leave is given you,— for a meal, (and then) not (so early as) to wait for its preparation: but when ye are invited, enter; and when ye have taken your meal, disperse, without seeking familiar talk. Such (behaviour) annoys the Prophet: he is ashamed to dismiss you, but Allāh is not ashamed (to tell you) the truth. And when ye ask (his ladies) for anything ye want, ask them from before a screen: that makes for greater purity for your hearts and for theirs. Nor is it right for you that ye should annoy Allāh's Messenger, or that ye should marry his widows after him at any time. Truly such a thing is in Allāh's sight an enormity. (Al-Qur'an, 033.05, Al-Ahzab (The Clans, the Coalition, the Combined Forces)]

2.6.10 Physical and Mental Cleanliness

Knowledge and bodily strength are better than abundant riches. Purity in body, mind and hearts. Health and Cleanliness should be taken care of.

لا تَقُمْ فِيهِ أَبَدًا لَمَسْجِدٌ أُسِّسَ عَلَى التَّقْوَى مِنْ أَوَّلِ يَوْمٍ أَحَقُّ أَنْ تَقُومَ فِيهِ فِيهِ رِجَالٌ يُحِبُّونَ أَنْ يَتَطَهَّرُوا وَاللَّهُ يُحِبُّ الْمُطَّهِّرِينَ

Never stand thou forth therein. There is a mosque whose foundation was laid from the first day on piety; it is more worthy of the standing forth (for prayer) therein. In it are men who love to be purified; and Allāh loveth those who make themselves pure. [Al-Qur'an, 009.10, At-Tawba (Repentance, Dispensation)]

يَا أَيُّهَا الَّذِينَ آمَنُوا لا تَقْرَبُوا الصَّلاةَ وَأَنْتُمْ سُكَارَى حَتَّى تَعْلَمُوا مَا تَقُولُونَ وَلا جُنُبًا إِلا عَابِرِي سَبِيلٍ حَتَّى تَغْتَسِلُوا وَإِنْ كُنْتُمْ مَرْضَى أَوْ عَلَى سَفَرٍ أَوْ جَاءَ أَحَدٌ مِنْكُمْ مِنَ الْغَائِطِ أَوْ لامَسْتُمُ النِّسَاءَ فَلَمْ تَجِدُوا مَاءً فَتَيَمَّمُوا صَعِيدًا طَيِّبًا فَامْسَحُوا بِوُجُوهِكُمْ وَأَيْدِيكُمْ إِنَّ اللَّهَ كَانَ عَفُوًّا غَفُورًا

O ye who believe! Approach not prayers with a mind befogged, until ye can understand all that ye say,—nor in a state of ceremonial impurity (Except when travelling on the road), until after washing your whole body. If ye are ill, or on a journey, or one of you cometh from offices of nature, or ye have been in contact with women, and ye find no water, then take for yourselves clean sand or earth, and rub therewith your faces and hands. For Allāh doth blot out sins and forgive again and again. (Al-Qur'an, 004.04, An-Nisa (Women)]

يَا أَيُّهَا الَّذِينَ آمَنُوا إِذَا قُمْتُمْ إِلَى الصَّلاةِ فَاغْسِلُوا وُجُوهَكُمْ وَأَيْدِيَكُمْ إِلَى الْمَرَافِقِ وَامْسَحُوا بِرُءُوسِكُمْ وَأَرْجُلَكُمْ إِلَى الْكَعْبَيْنِ وَإِنْ كُنْتُمْ جُنُبًا فَاطَّهَّرُوا وَإِنْ كُنْتُمْ مَرْضَى أَوْ عَلَى سَفَرٍ أَوْ جَاءَ أَحَدٌ مِنْكُمْ مِنَ الْغَائِطِ أَوْ لامَسْتُمُ النِّسَاءَ فَلَمْ تَجِدُوا مَاءً فَتَيَمَّمُوا صَعِيدًا طَيِّبًا فَامْسَحُوا بِوُجُوهِكُمْ وَأَيْدِيكُمْ مِنْهُ مَا يُرِيدُ اللَّهُ لِيَجْعَلَ عَلَيْكُمْ مِنْ حَرَجٍ وَلَكِنْ يُرِيدُ لِيُطَهِّرَكُمْ وَلِيُتِمَّ نِعْمَتَهُ عَلَيْكُمْ لَعَلَّكُمْ تَشْكُرُونَ

O ye who believe! when ye prepare for prayer, wash your faces, and your hands (and arms) to the elbows; Rub your heads (with water); and (wash) your feet to the ankles. If ye are in a state of ceremonial impurity, bathe your whole body. But if ye are ill, or on a journey, or one of you cometh from offices of nature, or ye have been in contact with women, and ye find no water, then take for yourselves clean sand or earth, and rub therewith your faces and hands, Allāh doth not wish to place you in a difficulty, but to make you clean, and to complete his favour to you, that ye may be grateful. [Al-Qur'an, 005.00, Al-Maeda (The Table, The Table Spread)]

2.6.11. Manners of Eating and Drinking

Certain things as pork, wine etc. prohibited. Eat what is on earth, lawful and good. Eat and drink but waste not by excess, for Allāh loveth not the wasters. Squander not your wealth in the manner of a spendthrift.

إِنَّمَا حَرَّمَ عَلَيْكُمُ الْمَيْتَةَ وَالدَّمَ وَلَحْمَ الْخِنْزِيرِ وَمَا أُهِلَّ بِهِ لِغَيْرِ اللَّهِ فَمَنِ اضْطُرَّ غَيْرَ بَاغٍ وَلَا عَادٍ فَلَا إِثْمَ عَلَيْهِ إِنَّ اللَّهَ غَفُورٌ رَحِيمٌ

He hath only forbidden you dead meat, and blood, and the flesh of swine, and that on which any other name hath been invoked besides that of Allāh. But if one is forced by necessity, without wilful disobedience, nor transgressing due limits,—then is he guiltless. For Allāh is Oft-forgiving Most Merciful. (Al-Qur'an, 002.173 (Al-Baqara)]

يَا أَيُّهَا النَّاسُ كُلُوا مِمَّا فِي الْأَرْضِ حَلَالًا طَيِّبًا وَلَا تَتَّبِعُوا خُطُوَاتِ الشَّيْطَانِ إِنَّهُ لَكُمْ عَدُوٌّ مُبِينٌ

O ye people! Eat of what is on earth, Lawful and good; and do not follow the footsteps of the evil one, for he is to you an avowed enemy. [Al-Qur'an, 002.168 (Al-Baqara)]

يَا بَنِي آدَمَ خُذُوا زِينَتَكُمْ عِنْدَ كُلِّ مَسْجِدٍ وَكُلُوا وَاشْرَبُوا وَلَا تُسْرِفُوا إِنَّهُ لَا يُحِبُّ الْمُسْرِفِينَ

O Children of Adam! wear your beautiful apparel at every time and place of prayer: eat and drink: But waste not by excess, for Allāh loveth not the wasters. [Al-Qur'an, 007.03, Al-Araf (The Heights)]

وَآتِ ذَا الْقُرْبَى حَقَّهُ وَالْمِسْكِينَ وَابْنَ السَّبِيلِ وَلَا تُبَذِّرْ تَبْذِيرًا

And render to the kindred their due rights, as (also) to those in want, and to the wayfarer: But squander not (your wealth) in the manner of a spendthrift. [Al-Qur'an, 017.026 (Al-Isra)]

2.6.12 Marital Relations

God has created mates and has put love and merry between you and your (hearts). Wives and offsprings are the comfort of our eyes. Men are the protectors and maintainers of women, because Allāh has given the one more (strength) than the other, and because they support them from their means. Therefore, the righteous women are devoutly obedient, and guard in (the husband's) absence what Allāh would have them guard.

وَمِنْ آيَاتِهِ أنْ خَلَقَ لكُمْ مِنْ أنْفُسِكُمْ أزْوَاجًا لِتَسْكُنُوا إِلَيْهَا وَجَعَلَ بَيْنَكُمْ مَوَدَّةً وَرَحْمَةً إِنَّ فِي ذَلِكَ لآيَاتٍ لِقَوْمٍ يَتَفَكَّرُونَ

And among His Signs is this, that He created for you mates from among yourselves, that ye may dwell in tranquillity with them, and He has put love and mercy between your (hearts): verily in that are Signs for those who reflect. [Al-Qur'an, 030.021 (Ar-Room)]

وَالَّذِينَ يَقُولُونَ رَبَّنَا هَبْ لَنَا مِنْ أزْوَاجِنَا وَذُرِّيَّاتِنَا قُرَّةَ أعْيُنٍ وَاجْعَلْنَا لِلْمُتَّقِينَ إِمَامًا

And those who pray, "Our Lord! Grant unto us wives and offspring who will be the comfort of our eyes, and give us (the grace) to lead the righteous." [Al-Qur'an, 025.07, Al-Furqan (The Criterion, The Standard)]

2.6.13 Don't Assassinate Children

Kill not your children for fear of want: We shall provide sustenance for them as well as for you. Verily, the killing of them is a great sin. In some cases the demands of families may compel you to use unfair means in earning wealth. In such cases they are no less than enemies. And know ye that your possessions and your progeny are but a trial; and that it is Allāh with Whom lies your highest reward.

وَلَا تَقْتُلُوا أَوْلَادَكُمْ خَشْيَةَ إِمْلَاقٍ نَحْنُ نَرْزُقُهُمْ وَإِيَّاكُمْ إِنَّ قَتْلَهُمْ كَانَ خِطْئًا كَبِيرًا

Kill not your children for fear of want: We shall provide sustenance for them as well as for you. Verily the killing of them is a great sin. [Al-Qur'an, 017.031 (Al-Isra)]

وَاعْلَمُوا أَنَّمَا أَمْوَالُكُمْ وَأَوْلَادُكُمْ فِتْنَةٌ وَأَنَّ اللَّهَ عِنْدَهُ أَجْرٌ عَظِيمٌ

And know ye that your possessions and your progeny are but a trial; and that it is Allāh with Whom lies your highest reward. [Al-Qur'an, 008.02, Al-Anfal (Spoils of War, Booty)]

2.6.14 Due Regard to Parents

Be good to your parents. Be kind to parents. Do not rebuke your parents in their old age. Hether one or both of them attain old age in thy life, say not to them a word of contempt, nor repel them, but address them in terms of honour. And, out of kindness, lower to them the wing of humility, and say: "My Lord! Bestow on them thy Mercy even as they cherished me in childhood."

قُلْ تَعَالَوْا أَتْلُ مَا حَرَّمَ رَبُّكُمْ عَلَيْكُمْ أَلَا تُشْرِكُوا بِهِ شَيْئًا وَبِالْوَالِدَيْنِ إِحْسَانًا وَلَا تَقْتُلُوا أَوْلَادَكُمْ مِنْ إِمْلَاقٍ نَحْنُ نَرْزُقُكُمْ وَإِيَّاهُمْ وَلَا تَقْرَبُوا الْفَوَاحِشَ مَا ظَهَرَ مِنْهَا وَمَا بَطَنَ وَلَا تَقْتُلُوا النَّفْسَ الَّتِي حَرَّمَ اللَّهُ إِلَّا بِالْحَقِّ ذَلِكُمْ وَصَّاكُمْ بِهِ لَعَلَّكُمْ تَعْقِلُونَ

Say: "Come, I will rehearse what Allāh hath (really) prohibited you from": Join not anything as equal with Him; be good to your parents; kill not your children on a plea of want;—We provide sustenance for you and for them;—come not nigh to shameful deeds. Whether open or secret; take not life, which Allāh hath made sacred, except by way of justice and law: thus doth He command you, that ye may learn wisdom. [Al-Qur'an, 006.15, Al-Anaam (Cattle, Livestock)]

وَقَضَى رَبُّكَ أَلَا تَعْبُدُوا إِلَّا إِيَّاهُ وَبِالْوَالِدَيْنِ إِحْسَانًا إِمَّا يَبْلُغَنَّ عِنْدَكَ الْكِبَرَ أَحَدُهُمَا أَوْ كِلَاهُمَا فَلَا تَقُلْ لَهُمَا أُفٍّ وَلَا تَنْهَرْهُمَا وَقُلْ لَهُمَا قَوْلًا كَرِيمًا

Thy Lord hath decreed that ye worship none but Him, and that ye be kind to parents. Whether one or both of them attain old age in thy life, say not to them a word of contempt, nor repel them, but address them in terms of honour. [Al-Qur'an, 017.02, Al-Isra (Isra)]

وَاخْفِضْ لَهُمَا جَنَاحَ الذُّلِّ مِنَ الرَّحْمَةِ وَقُلْ رَبِّ ارْحَمْهُمَا كَمَا رَبَّيَانِي صَغِيرًا

And, out of kindness, lower to them the wing of humility, and say: "My Lord! bestow on them thy Mercy even as they cherished me in childhood." [Al-Qur'an, 017.024 (Al-Isra)]

2.6.15 Relation with Relatives and Orphans

Treat with kindness your parents and kindred, and orphans and those in need; speak fair to the people; be steadfast in prayer; and practise regular charity. We should love our relatives and help them in need.

وَإِذْ أَخَذْنَا مِيثَاقَ بَنِي إِسْرَائِيلَ لا تَعْبُدُونَ إِلا اللَّهَ وَبِالْوَالِدَيْنِ إِحْسَانًا وَذِي الْقُرْبَى وَالْيَتَامَى وَالْمَسَاكِينِ وَقُولُوا لِلنَّاسِ حُسْنًا وَأَقِيمُوا الصَّلاةَ وَآتُوا الزَّكَاةَ ثُمَّ تَوَلَّيْتُمْ إِلا قَلِيلا مِنْكُمْ وَأَنْتُمْ مُعْرِضُونَ

And remember We took a covenant from the Children of Israel (to this effect): Worship none but Allāh; treat with kindness your parents and kindred, and orphans and those in need; speak fair to the people; be steadfast in prayer; and practise regular charity. Then did ye turn back, except a few among you, and ye backslide (even now). [Al-Qur'an, 002.083 (Al-Baqara)]

لَيْسَ الْبِرَّ أَنْ تُوَلُّوا وُجُوهَكُمْ قِبَلَ الْمَشْرِقِ وَالْمَغْرِبِ وَلَكِنَّ الْبِرَّ مَنْ آمَنَ بِاللَّهِ وَالْيَوْمِ الآخِرِ وَالْمَلائِكَةِ وَالْكِتَابِ وَالنَّبِيِّينَ وَآتَى الْمَالَ عَلَى حُبِّهِ ذَوِي الْقُرْبَى وَالْيَتَامَى وَالْمَسَاكِينَ وَابْنَ السَّبِيلِ وَالسَّائِلِينَ وَفِي الرِّقَابِ وَأَقَامَ الصَّلاةَ وَآتَى الزَّكَاةَ وَالْمُوفُونَ بِعَهْدِهِمْ إِذَا عَاهَدُوا وَالصَّابِرِينَ فِي الْبَأْسَاءِ وَالضَّرَّاءِ وَحِينَ الْبَأْسِ أُولَئِكَ الَّذِينَ صَدَقُوا وَأُولَئِكَ هُمُ الْمُتَّقُونَ

It is not righteousness that ye turn your faces Towards east or West; but it is righteousness—to believe in Allāh and the Last Day, and the Angels, and the Book, and the Messengers; to spend of your substance, out of love for Him, for your kin, for orphans, for the needy, for the wayfarer, for those who ask, and for the ransom of slaves; to be steadfast in prayer, and practice regular charity; to fulfil the contracts which ye have made; and to be firm and patient, in pain (or suffering) and adversity, and throughout all periods of panic. Such are the people of truth, the Allāh -fearing. [Al-Qur'an, 002.17, Al-Baqara (The Cow)]

2.6.16 Behaviour with Neighbours and Friends

Do good to neighbours and friends.

وَاعْبُدُوا اللهَ وَلا تُشْرِكُوا بِهِ شَيْئًا وَبِالْوَالِدَيْنِ إِحْسَانًا وَبِذِي الْقُرْبَى وَالْيَتَامَى
وَالْمَسَاكِينِ وَالْجَارِ ذِي الْقُرْبَى وَالْجَارِ الْجُنُبِ وَالصَّاحِبِ بِالْجَنْبِ وَابْنِ
السَّبِيلِ وَمَا مَلَكَتْ أَيْمَانُكُمْ إِنَّ اللهَ لا يُحِبُّ مَنْ كَانَ مُخْتَالا فَخُورًا

Serve Allāh, and join not any partners with Him; and do good—to parents, kinsfolk, orphans, those in need, neighbours who are near, neighbours who are strangers, the companion by your side, the wayfarer (ye meet), and what your right hands possess: For Allāh loveth not the arrogant, the vainglorious. (Al-Qur'an, 004.036 (An-Nisa)]

2.6.17 Treatment with Orphan

Not only help but also honour the orphan. Treat not the orphan with harshness.

فَأَمَّا الْيَتِيمَ فَلا تَقْهَرْ

Therefore, treat not the orphan with harshness. (Al-Qur'an, 093.00, Ad-Dhuha (The Morning Hours, Morning Bright)]

2.6.18 Behaviour with the Needy and Deprived

Treat with kindness those in need. In the wealth and possessions is the right of the needy. Kind words and covering of faults are better than charity.

وَفِي أَمْوَالِهِمْ حَقٌّ لِلسَّائِلِ وَالْمَحْرُومِ

And in their wealth and possessions (was remembered) the right of the (needy) him who asked, and him who (for some reason) was prevented (from asking). (Al-Qur'an, 051.01, Adh-Dhariyat (The Winnowing winds)]

وَإِذْ أَخَذْنَا مِيثَاقَكُمْ وَرَفَعْنَا فَوْقَكُمُ الطُّورَ خُذُوا مَا آتَيْنَاكُمْ بِقُوَّةٍ وَاذْكُرُوا مَا فِيهِ لَعَلَّكُمْ تَتَّقُونَ

And remember We took your covenant and We raised above you (The towering height) of Mount (Sinai): (Saying): "Hold firmly to what We have given you and bring (ever) to remembrance what is therein: Perchance ye may fear Allāh." [Al-Qur'an, 002.063 (Al-Baqara)]

2.6.19 Manners of Dealing with Credits

Usury is forbidden. Introduce to writing transactions involving future obligations

الَّذِينَ يَأْكُلُونَ الرِّبَا لا يَقُومُونَ إِلا كَمَا يَقُومُ الَّذِي يَتَخَبَّطُهُ الشَّيْطَانُ مِنَ الْمَسِّ ذَلِكَ بِأَنَّهُمْ قَالُوا إِنَّمَا الْبَيْعُ مِثْلُ الرِّبَا وَأَحَلَّ اللَّهُ الْبَيْعَ وَحَرَّمَ الرِّبَا فَمَنْ جَاءَهُ مَوْعِظَةٌ مِنْ رَبِّهِ فَانْتَهَى فَلَهُ مَا سَلَفَ وَأَمْرُهُ إِلَى اللَّهِ وَمَنْ عَادَ فَأُولَئِكَ أَصْحَابُ النَّارِ هُمْ فِيهَا خَالِدُونَ

Those who devour usury will not stand except as stand one whom the Evil one by his touch Hath driven to madness. That is because they say: "Trade is like usury," but Allāh hath permitted trade and forbidden usury. Those who after receiving direction from their Lord, desist, shall be pardoned for the past; their case is for Allāh (to judge); but those who repeat (The offence) are companions of the Fire: They will abide therein (for ever). (Al-Qur'an, 002.27, Al-Baqara)]

وَالَّذِينَ آمَنُوا وَعَمِلُوا الصَّالِحَاتِ أُولَئِكَ أَصْحَابُ الْجَنَّةِ هُمْ فِيهَا خَالِدُونَ

O ye who believe! When ye deal with each other, in transactions involving future obligations in a fixed period of time, reduce them to writing. Let a scribe write down faithfully as between the parties: let not the scribe refuse to write: as Allāh Has taught him, so let him write. Let him who incurs the liability dictate, but let him fear His Lord Allāh, and not diminish aught of what he owes. If they party liable is mentally deficient, or weak, or unable Himself to dictate, Let his guardian dictate faithfully, and get two witnesses, out of your own men, and if there are not two men, then a man and two women, such as ye choose, for witnesses, so that if one of them errs, the other can remind her. The witnesses should not refuse when they are called on (For evidence). Disdain not to reduce to writing (your contract) for a future period, whether it be small or big: it is juster in the sight of Allāh, More suitable as evidence, and more convenient to prevent doubts among yourselves, but if it be a transaction which ye carry out on the spot among yourselves, there is no blame on you if ye reduce it not to writing. But take witness whenever ye make a commercial contract; and let neither scribe nor witness suffer harm. If ye do (such harm), it would be wickedness in you. So fear Allāh; For it is Allāh that teaches you. And Allāh is well acquainted with all things. [Al-Qur'an, 002.28, Al-Baqara (The Cow)]

2.6.20 Keeping Promises

Keep your promises and fulfil obligations.

إِنَّ اللَّهَ يَأْمُرُكُمْ أَنْ تُؤَدُّوا الأَمَانَاتِ إِلَى أَهْلِهَا وَإِذَا حَكَمْتُمْ بَيْنَ النَّاسِ أَنْ
تَحْكُمُوا بِالْعَدْلِ إِنَّ اللَّهَ نِعِمَّا يَعِظُكُمْ بِهِ إِنَّ اللَّهَ كَانَ سَمِيعًا بَصِيرًا

Allāh doth command you to render back your Trusts to those to whom they are due; And when ye judge between man and man, that ye judge with justice: Verily how excellent is the teaching which He giveth you! For Allāh is He Who heareth and seeth all things. [Al-Qur'an, 004.058 (An-Nisa)]

2.6.21 Miscellaneous

(a) Help one another in acts of righteousness and piety, but not in sin and rencour.

(b) Swell not your cheek at men.

وَلا تُصَعِّرْ خَدَّكَ لِلنَّاسِ وَلا تَمْشِ فِي الأَرْضِ مَرَحًا إِنَّ اللهَ لا يُحِبُّ كُلَّ مُخْتَالٍ فَخُورٍ

"And swell not thy cheek (for pride) at men, nor walk in insolence through the earth; for Allāh loveth not any arrogant boaster. [Al-Qur'an, 031.01, Luqman (Luqman)]

(c) Do not enjoin right conduct on the people and forget to practice it yourselves.

أَتَأْمُرُونَ النَّاسَ بِالْبِرِّ وَتَنسَوْنَ أَنفُسَكُمْ وَأَنتُمْ تَتْلُونَ الْكِتَابَ أَفَلا تَعْقِلُونَ

Do ye enjoin right conduct on the people, and forget (To practise it) yourselves, and yet ye study the Scripture? Will ye not understand? [Al-Qur'an, 002.044 (Al-Baqara)]

(d) When you have taken a decision, pur your trust in Allāh.

فَبِمَا رَحْمَةٍ مِنَ اللهِ لِنْتَ لَهُمْ وَلَوْ كُنْتَ فَظًا غَلِيظَ الْقَلْبِ لانْفَضُّوا مِنْ حَوْلِكَ فَاعْفُ عَنْهُمْ وَاسْتَغْفِرْ لَهُمْ وَشَاوِرْهُمْ فِي الأَمْرِ فَإِذَا عَزَمْتَ فَتَوَكَّلْ عَلَى اللهِ إِنَّ اللهَ يُحِبُّ الْمُتَوَكِّلِينَ

It is part of the Mercy of Allāh that thou dost deal gently with them Wert thou severe or harsh-hearted, they would have broken away from about thee: so pass over (Their faults), and ask for (Allāh's) forgiveness for them; and consult them in affairs (of moment). Then, when thou hast Taken a decision put thy trust in Allāh. For Allāh loves those who put their trust (in Him). [Al-Qur'an, 003.15, Aal-E-Imran (The Family of Imran)]

(e) Never be hypocritical saying with lips that is not in hearts.

وَلِيَعْلَمَ الَّذِينَ نَافَقُوا وَقِيلَ لَهُمْ تَعَالَوْا قَاتِلُوا فِي سَبِيلِ اللَّهِ أَوِ ادْفَعُوا قَالُوا لَوْ نَعْلَمُ قِتَالًا لَاتَّبَعْنَاكُمْ هُمْ لِلْكُفْرِ يَوْمَئِذٍ أَقْرَبُ مِنْهُمْ لِلْإِيمَانِ يَقُولُونَ بِأَفْوَاهِهِمْ مَا لَيْسَ فِي قُلُوبِهِمْ وَاللَّهُ أَعْلَمُ بِمَا يَكْتُمُونَ

And the Hypocrites also. These were told: "Come, fight in the way of Allāh, or (at least) drive (The foe from your city)." They said: "Had we known how to fight, we should certainly have followed you." They were that day nearer to Unbelief than to Faith, saying with their lips what was not in their hearts but Allāh hath full knowledge of all they conceal. [Al-Qur'an, 003.167 (Aal-E-Imran)]

(f) Avoid Conjecturing

وَإِنْ تُطِعْ أَكْثَرَ مَنْ فِي الْأَرْضِ يُضِلُّوكَ عَنْ سَبِيلِ اللَّهِ إِنْ يَتَّبِعُونَ إِلَّا الظَّنَّ وَإِنْ هُمْ إِلَّا يَخْرُصُونَ

[Al-Qur'an, 006.116 (Al-Anaam)]

The Holy Qur'an is meant for humanity's welfare; therefore, each and every word of it is with reference to 'man' and his uplift. Thus, its simple commands and prohibitions, its higher philosophical subjects, its permanenet values, its lists of human rights and obligations, all conduce to man's evolution from his animality to the higher stages of spirituality.

3
Critical Analysis of the Content according to the Objectives

3.1 First Objective of the Study is—To Analyse the Duties and Characteristics of the Teacher mentioned according to the Message of Qur'an

The success of education depends as much on the skilful teaching of the subjects as on the fitness of the curriculum. Much depends on the teacher himself. It is the personality of the teacher, his efficiency and superior human qualities that influence the intellectual and the spiritual growth of the child. A teacher is not a man of mean status: he is a maker of men. He builds up children to fit in the general social frame and guides their destinies to their final goal.

Need of a Good Teacher

Prof. **Humayun Kabir** states: **"Without Good teachers, even the best of system is bound to fail. With good teachers, even the worst of system can be largely overcome."** There is need of really good teachers who have some unique qualities about them. In India we do not need such teachers who consider imparting of information to be their only duty. They are also expected to act as social reformer, moralist, nationalist, national integrator. The teacher is an important figure and he is expected to remain important. Study of Qur'an and *Hadith* is beneficial for the teachers because Qur'an contains an enormous range of topics. It tells us about God, His attributes, man's position in the universe, his aim in life and how to attain that aim, how we stand in relation to God and to our fellow-beings. It gives details of what one should believe and how it should be put into practice. The next life is described in it in full. Histories of previous nations and their prophets, as well as many events from the life of the Holy Prophet himself, are also given in the Qur'an. It gives arguments to disprove false beliefs of all kinds, and answers all sorts of questions and objections raised about its teachings and about the Holy Prophet. Guidance, laws and regulations on everyday subjects such as family life, business dealings, the law, war and peace, women's rights, hygiene, government and democracy etc., is also to be found in the Holy Book. When dealing with any topic, the Holy Qur'an gives reasons, arguments and evidence to support its teachings, and it challenges those who disagree with it to produce proof of their views.

The first step in the education of mankind was initiated by Allāh Himself – the Absolute Source of all knowledge and wisdom. He taught Adam – the first human being on the earth – the names and knowledge of all things in the universe. [Al-Qur'an, 002.031 (Al-Baqara)]

This signifies the truth that man without knowledge of the world was not perfect and it was by virtue of this knowledge and wisdom, transmitted to him by his Creator, that he earned the dignified status of a human being. In order to educate the human race properly and perpetuate the system and practice of teaching He sent down His Prophets from time to time. The last and most perfect in the line is the Holy Prophet Muhammad (SAW).

According to wife of Muhammad, Aisha, **"He was a personification of the Qur'an."** That is to say, Muhammad molded his own life in accordance with the ideal pattern of life that he presented to others in the form of the Qur'an. Since a teacher is intended to mould a man's character, his mission is almost similar to that of a prophet; and he is a successor to the holy inheritance of knowledge and wisdom. Unless this divine legacy of human teaching and guidance is maintained and handed down justly, there should be little hope of achieving the good of mankind. Education, therefore, is a human necessity; it is not something which can be acquired by will or by wish, but it has to be achieved assiduously thought the medium of an ideal teacher.

An ideal teacher is necessarily a man of firm and unshakable faith in Allāh in all respects. **Faith (*Iman*);** which we know is the central pillar of Islam. He shows complete reliance on Him and in his every effort invokes His blessings, assistance and mercy for the fulfillment of his mission as a teacher. He is a man of very strong character, courage and confidence and therefore unstooping to intimidation and immoral pulls of the outside forces. ***Tauhid ur rabubiyah*,** the permanent value of the Qur'an teaches the same thing, i.e. the human 'self' is to be so perfected, individually as well as collectively. He does not let himself loose to be led away by the vicious influences of the society, but on the contrary, he always tries to eradicate its ills and vices.

Also he is quite conscious of his responsibilities to his Creator, his own self and to the people around him. **Bearing duties and responsibilities** is also permanent value of the Qur'an. He should be well aware of his duties. He must feel morally responsible to accept his weaknesses and failures. This moral courage is a big step towards self-correction and repentance. A teacher should know his weaknesses and improve them. He should not hesitate and feel shame in accepting his weaknesses and should correct himself timely. He should not teach the students if he is weak in his subject. He should first of all master the subject and remove all the weakness then proceed towards teaching.

Justice which is very important value of the Holy Qur'an should be an important value of a teacher also. In a society in which justice is not practiced in daily affairs nothing remains in its proper place. Wrong placing of things means loss of equilibrium, imbalance, unevenness, inequality and disturbance in right proportion. By having this quality, a teacher can do justice with his students; he is able to remove the feelings of selfishness or attraction. The intrinsic worth of a man consists in his qualities of honesty, truthfulness and justice. According to Qur'an a man should stand out firmly for justice, even as against yourselves, or your parents, or your kin, and whether it is (against) rich or poor. He should not follow the lust of his hearts. This is the highest quality of a person.

Charity or *Zakat* is the permanent value of the Qur'an as well as amongst the five pillars of Islam. A teacher should have this quality to remove the differences amongst his students. He should know that although all human beings are created alike, their fortunes and resources vary in quality and extent. Some are rich and abundantly resourceful and some happen to be poor and helpless. These individual differences are quite significant as they have been made the cause of mutual sympathy and kindness and keeping people attached to each other and united. A teacher can also remove individual differences regarding rich and poor amongst his students. Allāh has obliged the well to do and prosperous people to help the poor and helpless humanity without any selfish motives or causing any grief and disgrace to them, in order to banish poverty and destitution from the society as well as to establish bonds of love and fraternity among the people. He can teach his students as well as their parents who make a boastful display and pretence of their kindness and magnanimity and keep trumpeting what a little bit they for others for earning public appreciation and impressing upon the beneficiaries that but for their favour and mercy they would face hardship and misery and thus they hurt their feeling and make them awfully aggrieved humiliated with such a selfishly motivated and agonizing gesture of sympathy support, Allāh is greatly displeased with such people. He should teach that dispensation of alms and charity must be done voluntarily and as a moral obligation, and not with intent to exact return service or expression of gratitude. Wealth must constantly remain in circulation; its stoppage anywhere and in any form is harmful to the concept of a classless society because it gives rise to want and scarcity—the deadliest enemies of man's security, dignity and honour.

According to Qur'an **Wealth should be fully utilized.** It

should not be wasted. Although a man's act of spending money and wealth is his personal concern and he has a legitimate right to utilize it without fear or hesitation, it is certainly not meant for being wasted want only and in wrongful pursuits, not for hatching trouble for the mankind, spreading corruption or making mischief in the earth. Such a willful act often leads to poverty and sin. A man is obliged to earn his living by lawful means and spend his money in lawful ways and whatever he can spare he may help out of it those who may be distressed and rightly deserving. A teacher can effectively inculcate in the young minds the feelings of sympathy and love for the mankind in general and for the poor and afflicted in particular and teach them how best they can administer alms and charity out of what is lawful and pure and make legitimate use of their wealth and property.

Regard for Humanity which is another permanent value of the Holy Qur'an should be a permanent value of teacher also. A teacher should show due regard to every child. It will raise his status here. The teacher is to handle the child in order to educate him. He is just like an artist who should exploit different things contained in the child for achieving the educational ends. The success of education depends on the cooperation between the teacher and the taught. For this cooperation the teacher should respect the individuality of the child and he in turn will have all the regards for him. Nothing can be imposed on the child.

The Qur'an gives the teaching of **unification of mankind and freedom**. No philosophy can be sound for educational purposes without having the unity of mankind as its core. The Message of Allāh has always been for maintaining this unity. Differences spring up between individuals and nations through selfishness and egotism. Respect for humanity is possible only when we think in terms of the oneness of its origin. It is very important for a teacher to maintain unity amongst his class, students of the school. Qur'an does not insist on imposing one's thoughts on others. Man is free to choose between right and wrong. A teacher should also not make to accept the truth or ideologies by force, but should give the students proper reasons and examples as are given in Qur'an. For every value or behaviour adoption, there is proper reason and various examples are given in Qur'an.

The most glorifying deed of a true human being is his **selfless service** and doing good to making irrespective of the considerations of the caste, creed or kinship. Since man by nature is good he is supposed to maintain that goodness as a teacher and develop it to the height of perfection; and in that respect he should avoid all temptations and trends of behaviour likely to damage the nobility of his nature. It is a great sin to conspire out of jealousy and ill will to harm someone and damage his honour. A teacher should remove such type of habits from his students.

Fulfillment of agreement or **keeping promise** is very essential value of the Qur'an. A teacher should teach his students to keep their promises. Since people live in a society they depend upon mutual help and cooperation. They make dealings with each other and in that respect they enter into agreements and make promises on oath. Making promises or swearing is very easy, but fulfillment of the commitments made is rather a burdensome affair. Making a promise means that a person undertakes to do a particular thing or a job. In case promises or agreements made are not honoured the persons affected get disappointed and they lose trust in each other; and if there exists no mutual trust and understanding there can never exist any good will and amity. Consequently, the humanity which is a distinct and super most creation on the earth will sunder into disgruntled factions bringing about universal hatred and chaos. The promises made are often authenticated by swearing as a sign of solemn undertaking, yet such undertakings are sometimes ignored and flouted. Certain people especially young children develop a loose habit of swearing; their statements and utterances are frequently and thoughtlessly attested by oaths which carry little significance and credibility. This habit must be discouraged and got rid of in their early stages.

Individual effort is insisted in Qur'an and it has been adopted in the life style by Prophet Muhammad (SAW). He is the live example of self-effort and struggle. A teacher should also take pains in teaching the students. He should create himself as an example as students make teacher as his ideal and imitates him. He should teach the students to strive constantly, persistently and with perseverance to achieve a goal. To sit still in wait for something extraordinary to happen from outsides, is to invite death. Nations that become so self-satisfied and arrogant that they forget the spirit of God's guidance call their own destruction.

The Holy Qur'an is, indeed, a wonderful book: it is exactly what a book of right guidance ought to be. It throws light on complex problems of the Universe on the one hand, and gives guidance in respect of very important problems of human life on the other. It gives us the permanent values of life, which form the very foundation of education and culture, as well as directions about the everyday civic life of a man. So a teacher should go through the Holy Qur'an and teach its values and principles to the students also. Man's common relationships are the foundations on which big civilizations are not only built, but with the members of our family, with friends, with neighbours, with relatives, with common acquaintances, with foreigners, also what our mode of living, walking about eating and drinking, talking with each other and in gatherings etc. should be. A teacher builds a nation. National character is reflected from these common behaviours. Qur'an is a complete guide to develop whole personality of an individual. Individual can's stray from his path if he has gone through the teachings of Qur'an and *Hadith* thoroughly.

About **mutual contacts** Qur'an says that greetings should be done from both the sides. This is taught in the school as well as by the parents. According to Qur'an conversation should be done in a straight forward manner. No diplomism and circumlocution should be there. Truth should not be concealed and conversation should be done in a language which is known by most of the people. A teacher should also use the language which is easily understandable by the students. He should explain the subject matter in a straight forward manner so that the students have no problem in understanding. He should not use harsh sounds; he should be moderate and low in his tone.

According to Qur'an a man should not walk in insolence through the earth; for Allāh **loves not the arrogant boaster**. A person should wear simple and descent clothes. Show off must not be there. A teacher should put on simple, dignified, civilized dress and spend moderately on clothes. Holy Prophet says suggests avoiding luxury and extravagant finance in matters of dress. They should not show proud in their walking. Persons should not speak ill of each other behind their backs. It is like eating flesh of one's brother. A teacher should especially not adopt the quality of speaking ill of others in their back. We should wear a dress which covers and protects our body and meets the requirements of modesty, honour and virtue. Dress should also be an expression of culture, elegance and beauty. Women should not wear thin dress which should make their forms visible, not should they put on a tightly fitting dress which might make their figures prominent and alluring. The Holy Prophet Muhammad (SAW) has warned such immodest women of dire punishment.

The Holy Qur'an is meant for **humanity's welfare**; therefore, each and every word of it is with reference to 'man' and his uplift. Thus, its simple commands and prohibitions, its higher philosophical subjects, its permanent values, its lists of human rights and obligations, all conduce to man's evolution from his animalism to the higher stages of spirituality. A teacher should adopt permanent values and common manners taught by the Qur'an and *Hadith*. He should be an ideal of the students.

3.2 Second Objective of the Study is – To Study Guidance and Preaching of the Qur'an which could be Helpful for the Students

The qualities and attributes a learner is expected to inculcate into his personality are as follows:

In order to maintain the **external neatness and the internal purity**, the Prophet Muhammad said, "that neatness and purity are the foundations of Islam." According to this instruction the dress of the learner, the place where he studies the educative material he uses, are not only required to be clean, but his heart too should be clean from the evil desires which may disturb him and create negative emotions like anger lasciviousness, malice and haughtiness. It is expected that the learner should minimize, as much as possible, his other preoccupations other than those concerned with learning. Al-Ghazali says: knowledge will not surrender itself to the learner unless the wholly entrusts himself to knowledge. Thus, for him who is engaged in the pursuit of knowledge it is necessary to seek it at all times to do so from the cradle to the grave. The intermission and break in learning is a loss to the learner.

The **learner should pay high regard to his teacher**. Al-Ghazali says the learner is a patient and the educator is his physician. The teacher knows the mental level of his students. He decides accordingly as to what should be taught and what should not be taught. Posing unnecessary questions and speaking without permission create difficulties in the pursuit of knowledge. Sometimes the learner even fails in his mission of acquiring knowledge. Thus, the learner should not make haste but should proceed slowly and patiently. Moreover, he must inculcate in him self the attributes of solemnity, mildness and the fear of Allāh.

Silence has been lavishly praised in *Hadith*. It is related that one who keeps silence gets salvation. Believers have been asked either to utter good words or to keep silent. No doubt silence and concentration are necessary conditions for the acquisition of knowledge from the learned. The freedom of expression of views should not however be curtailed. The questions arising in the mind of a learner, if not properly answered can not satisfy his passion for knowledge. It is also related that the learner should join the company of scholars other than his teacher so that he may be aware of his teacher's deficiencies. On the other hand teachers are expected not to encroach into fields not known to them.

It is said that the **learned are the physicians of the society** and that wealth is the ailment of the society. If a physician himself becomes sick who will cure the ailing. It is pointed out to the learner not to hanker after wealth because wealth and its avariciousness create obstacles in the way of knowledge. It appears from the study of the Qur'an that the axiom of knowledge for the sake of knowledge and acquisition of knowledge for personal ends is not desirable in Islam. The Qur'an men exhort to acquire knowledge and to practice it. It is said that there were scholars who were depressed at the attitude of common folk towards knowledge and they urged their students to acquire knowledge for persona benefit. But this vies does not appear to be correct in the light of the clear exhortations of the Qur'an and the *Hadith*. The Qur'an says that the persons who conceal Divine Knowledge are guilty of gross crime. Thus, the learner is expected to transmit his acquired knowledge to those who are ignorant of it. To sum up, the learners are expected to maintain external neatness as well as internal purity.

A learner or a child should be **obedient and should respect his parents. It is next to worship of** Allāh. Allāh, is no doubt, is the Creator of the whole humanity, bit it is the parents who are the source of the physical emergence of man in the world. He child is born of his parents. His mother, from the time of conception to his birth, bears his troublesome and painful burden with utmost care and anxiety and suffers the pangs of delivery with patience and optimism. After his birth she feeds, nurses and tends him with maternal concern and affection at the cost of her own comforts and pleasures of life. His father exerts to procure things for his physical and intellectual demands. His home is his first school and nursery, where he learns to grow and mature physically, intellectually, morally, spiritually, economically and socially. Until his full-fledged maturity, he is entirely dependent on his parents. The child is wholly indebted to his parents for their exclusive parental love and care. So, the task of education should be to make him conscious of that indebtedness and his responsibility to them and teach him to show his filial obedience and respect to and humble himself before them in service and gratitude. The Qur'an strongly enjoins on the youth to treat their parents with kindness and reverence and look after them with devotion and dutifulness particularly in their days of old age and infirmity, and also keep on praying for their sound health and happiness.

Spying and backbiting are like eating one's brother's flesh according to Qur'an. Learners should remain away from such ill habits. It is the need of the day, as now a day's both teachers and students are involved in it. Every body wants to go ahead, but no body wants to work hard for it. He wants to make a good image of himself by speaking ill of others and good of one. Such a trend should definitely be removed. We have seen generally parents and friends call the children by their nick names. We should not call each other by offensive nick names. Students should also not be **jealous** of each other. They should not envy others for what Allāh has given them of His bounty. Students should work very hard for making their personality good and also for their studies.

Students should be taught the **common manners** as taught in the Qur'an as one would not enter any one's house without permission. They should not eat the things which are prohibited and which are bad for the health as we know knowledge and bodily strength are better than abundant riches. They should eat in sufficient quantity, but should not waste any thing. In the same way extravagancy is also not good. They should spend money on the things of need, but should not waste money on unnecessary things. They should be good in behaviour as well as friends. They should be taught to speak in a general language and should speak fair to the people. Tone of the voice should be low. They should not come near shameful deeds, whether open or secret. Vain talks should be avoided; listening to vain talks is also not fair. Shameful deeds should also be avoided. They should not walk on the earth in insolence and pride and should be moderate in their pace. Their walk should show humility and girls walk should walk bashfully. Children should be taught in manners to greet each other as taught in Qur'an. Greetings should be offered when one enter their own houses as well as others houses and even if an ignorant man addresses us.

There is a saying come down from ages that if wealth is lost, nothing is lost, if health is lost, something is lost, but if character is lost, everything is lost. One of the principal aims of education is the formation of **good character**. It is this outstanding quality of character that distinguishes man from the rest of creatures in the universe and elevates him in rank and glory. The best and most suitable period for character formation is the childhood – the age of growth and impression. Tribes, races and nations spring from the node of human stem; and this node is the childhood from which the whole humanity proceeds. So, the childhood is of paramount importance as in that period the foundation of future manhood is laid. So, in childhood of a student character building is most important function of teachers as well as parents.

3.3 Third Objective of the Study is – To Study the Role of Qur'an and Preaching of Prophet for the Benefit of the Society

A family unit normally consists of a group of persons, closely bound in blood relationship, such as parents and children. For living in a family each individual person has certain obligations to fulfil. The foremost among them is the expression and virtual demonstration of mutual respect, love and affection. Each person has to work for the collective good and welfare of the family to consolidate its strength and lay a firm foundation for the strong social structure and avoid all such activities which may tend to create prejudices against one another, cause quarrels, defile the sanctity of home and ultimately disrupt the unit. Such a spirit will keep a family happy and united for enjoying an honourable existence in the society. A child's immediate surroundings are his home, his village or home town and the people in which he moves and sets up contacts. He has therefore to learn how to live at home in a family and build up amicable and durable associations with the people around him so that he can make his domestic and social relationship congenial to his interests and aspirations and make a wholesome contribution to the development of his community and his nation. Progress of a society depends considerably on its teachers and students. The nation's well being depends on teacher's well being. No society can afford to neglect him. The teacher, above all, is the social engineer and social worker. He is the maker of the history; he is the maker of the society.

One of the effective ways of making a man feel indebted to his kindered and fellow beings **and show his respect to them** is to create in him a consciousness that his comfortable existence in the world is due to their contribution of effort and good will. Man cannot live in complete isolation from the rest of mankind, because he necessarily depends on their help and support for the successful accomplishment of his affairs and convenient solution of his problems of life. He gets comfort because other toil for him, he holds good social status because others respect him and he gains popularity and fame because others eulogize him. But for the understanding and cooperation of other people of his community or society it would be almost impossible for him to get on with the world amicably and his existence would rather be difficult and obscure. The Qur'an has enforced an etiquette which has definitely a far reaching influence in establishing cordial relations and brotherhood. It lays down that when a man meets any of his fellow men or comes across any stranger he should greet him with good wishes of peace and protection from evil; and if he is greeted by others he must make a return gesture in a similar or in a better form. This simple and auspicious form of reciprocating blessings and good wishes lays the foundations for future contacts and associations of benevolent nature. A man should also be grateful to his kindered, friends and fellow men for their goodness and favour done to him. Nothing is more unpleasant and annoying of a man than his indifference and irresponsiveness in respect of his expression of gratitude.

It is laid down in the Qur'an that children in a family, whether young or grown up, should not be allowed to be slipshod and vulgar in their talk, dress and manners, lest they should get into bad habits eventually. For creating in them reverence for their parents it is strictly forbidden for them to enter into their parents' chamber at three times in a day and night without asking for their permission and they should not feel shy of making such an approach before the morning prayer time, at non-time and after the night prayers, because these are the timings of their leisure and privacy. It is a marvelous principle indeed. It is intended to develop in the children a strong sense of morality and consideration for the personal rights and privileges in a **home** and **social discipline.**

The Qur'an prevents from unauthorized entry into a house other than one's own, unless and until one seeks permission from its inmates to enter, and on entrance he should meet them with greetings and blessings from Allāh. This kind of behaviour is significantly helpful in developing in the young children as well as in the adults a sense of **social respect** and **civic responsibility**. However, no bar has been placed on entering premises, which may be lying deserted and uninhabited, for the purpose of deriving some benefit from it.

For satisfaction of the natural human need man wears clothes to cover his shame and protect his body from injury, heat or cold. Clothes serve not only as a preservative, but also as an ornamental cover for the body which would otherwise look ugly and obscene. Ever since man has descended on the earth he has felt the need of keeping himself vestured, particularly those parts of his body which are delicate and need protection, and those which the human modesty requires, should remain shielded. Allāh has therefore provided man with necessary clothing. In utter disregard to this fundamental need of nature certain so called highly civilized races of the world favour nudity and prefer to remain nude or half nude. They erroneously believe that human development, moral as well as spiritual, can possibly be achieved in a state of complete nakedness. They plead that the natural nude human form, in which man has come into the world, has its own beauty, grace and charm and it provides a prime tonic of life. Such a view evidently presupposes that human nakedness may be always and freely exposed for public observation and appreciation for obtaining moral and spiritual satisfaction. But the Qur'an categorically condemns such an idea and strongly prevents from deriving any sensual pleasure from such an ugly and obscene sight. Allāh knows best the nature and weaknesses of man and has therefore ordained that he should be properly clad, particularly the women folk whose modesty is guarded in their clothes and not in the nakedness. As against the commandment of Allāh, the modern man has titled towards sex and his revolutionary bent of mind indicates without doubt to what low level of immorality he has fallen that what is vulgar and obscene, inhuman and sinful in the consideration of Allāh, is regarded by the audacious revolter as quite a human etiquette and a necessity. It is then the job of a teacher to impress on the young children that clothing is the nature's provision for the basic need of man, so they should **dress themselves decently** and adequately **to retain modesty as their virtue**; and this modesty, says Allāh, should further be fortified with piety to **maintain a true human value**.

Basically, man has been made of dust and he will revert to dust ultimately. In all fairness, therefore, he should be **humble** and unassuming in his manners and style. But the general observation is that when a man makes a good deal of fortune by hook or by crook and assumes a privileged status in social ranks he gets puffed up, becomes selfish and looks down upon his fellow beings who happen to have a bare living and lead a simple and hard life. A man's pride creates in him hatred and lack of sympathy and love for others, where as humility and the sense of mutual respect and sympathy refine the human feelings and bring about the social and national coherence. Allāh does not like those who are proud and selfish and He has ordained severe punishment for such people.

Certain manners in the young children and the youth are irritating; they humiliate man, so, they are **socially undesirable**. Some unpleasant features are: talking and laughing at a high pitch, walking too fast or too slow and extravagance and waste in eating and drinking. Normally, the behaviour with the people or the friends should be polite and respectful, pleasant and cheerful; it should be with a liberal mind, free from any kind of conceit or complex, irrespective of the sort of person or the people who may be addressed. The voice, when one talks, should be neither too high nor hoarse that it may irritate the hearer, not it should be too low that it becomes inaudible and needs repetition for understanding its meaning or purpose. Talking at a high pitch or speaking harshly has been compared to an unpleasant braying of an ass, and so it has been condemned in the Qur'an, because such behaviour lowers the dignity and grace of man.

The intrinsic worth of a man consists in his qualities of **honesty, truthfulness** and **justice**. In matters of dispute man must feel that he is a witness for Allāh, so, he should not follow passion lest he lapses and conceals the truth or mixes it with falsehood, not he should throw his own blame on others in order to absolve himself, his kin or his friends from a criminal involvement. Lying and hiding the truth is a worst sin which will not go unretributed. A truthful person is one who is honest and trustworthy. If he betrays the trust, misappropriates, wastes or eats away any trust property in his custody, he will surely deprive himself of his outstanding characteristic virtue. Allāh hates such people who are unreliable, fraudulent and treacherous.

Selfless service to mankind irrespective of the considerations of caste, creed or kinship is the most glorifying deed of a true human being. Those who do good are truly the faithful. It is a great sin to conspire out of jealousy and ill will to harm someone and damage his honour. Goodness may be shown even to those who may be the enemies, and by virtue of that goodness they could possibly turn out to be good friends. If harm is done to a man he would naturally like to avenge it. Vengeance may be justified only in case a person is wronged, but it must be with the limits laid as for the nature and the extent of the harm done. It would however be better for a person to show his goodness to endure the ills and forgive the wrong doers, and Allāh will compensate for it. Forgiveness in fact is an angelic nature; it breeds good-will and friendship, while retaliation is a devilish quality that creates lasting ill will and enmity.

Although all human beings are created alike, their fortunes and resources vary in quality and extent. Some are rich and abundantly resourceful and some happen to be poor and helpless. Allāh has therefore obliged the well to do and prosperous people to help the poor and helpless people without any selfish motives or causing any grief and disgrace to them, in order to banish poverty and destitution from the society as well as to establish bonds of love and fraternity among the people. **Charity** or

Zakat has been made compulsory on the eligible 'scheduled' (*sahibe Nisab*) persons. It awakens **a sense of social responsibility in man**, organizes human beings in a society and a state and enjoins the individual to subscribe to the **social good**. It also inculcates feelings of sympathy and love for the mankind in general and for the poor and afflicted in particular.

Since people live in a society they depend upon **mutual help and cooperation**. They make dealings with each other and in that respect they enter into agreements and make promises on oath. Qur'an teaches us that once a pledge is making or an undertaking is given it must be carried out. In case promises or agreements made or not honoured the persons affected get disappointed and they lose trust in each other and if there exists no mutual trust and understanding there can never exist any good will and amity. Consequently, the humanity which is a distinct and super most creation on the earth will sunder into disgruntled factions bringing about universal hatred and chaos.

The Qur'an also guides us to be **away form the bad company**. The popular adage: **"As the company so the colour"** is universally true. Man being a social creature is naturally inclined to have company of certain persons who may be holding homogeneous views and interests and with whom he can mix and converse freely. Companions can be good and bad. In a good company the associates are mostly cultured and friendly, they are an asset to the community, while a bad company includes idlers, rogues and unruly elements whose existence is always a threat to a peace loving society, because its influence is vicious and or criminal nature. Almost all evil habits and vices in the young children breed from their contacts with bad characters. A bad company is a positive source of all ills.

Certain ills and sinful acts are abominable; they are idolatry, murder, adultery, wine drinking and gambling. Idolatry is heinous act of defiance of the Supreme Authority of Allāh and an open challenge to Him. **Murder, adultery, wine drinking and gambling** also are the **wicked deeds,** which generate prolonged enmity and hatred among the people and destroy peace and tranquility in the world. It is therefore ordained that people should eschew these major sins for their own good and for the good of humanity at large. And Allāh, Who is Most Kind and Merciful, may probably condone their minor slips by virtue of their abstinence from the major vices.

A man's strength lies in his unity with his kinsfolk, friends and fellow men. A person, who does not enjoy confidence of his own people and has no cordial relations with them, cannot build up **ties of fraternity and friendship** with the other members of his society. Allāh gets angry with such people who do not fulfil their obligations towards their kinsfolk and other relatives and break with them on one pretext or another. It can be said with certitude that without the basic qualities of human character as described, a man or woman can never claim for an allotment of a place of honour in the world to come, which is as certain as death.

3.4 Fourth Objective of the Study is – To Study the Educational Implications of Qur'an

If we see the philosophical aspect of the Qur'an, i.e. Metaphysics, Axiology and Metaphysics of the Qur'an which has been discussed in Chapter – 4, we are able to know that Qur'an is not only a religious book, but it is a complete educational book also. Thus, it should be implied in our Education system also. It is Noble book of guidance for the welfare of the teachers, students and society. The Qur'an is the unique book. **It is the fountainhead of all knowledge and wisdom, the source of divine inspiration, the best and most reliable code of human code of human conduct and the only guide to truth and salvation.** It must be made the basis of all education and be made compulsory at all levels according to the requirements of age and comprehension, because **it teaches discipline and obedience,** and by virtue of it **human character gets sanctified and the correct sense of value is developed.** Every man and women, young and old is enjoined to study the Qur'an which provides substance for thought and research, examples and similitude's for understanding and directions and guidance for acts of goodness and piety. There is not a single essential principle or aspect of life which is not expounded in the Holy Book. Education must therefore inculcate in children all such habits and features which are positively good and rewarding, and which discourage and prevent them from intentions and deeds which are illicit and harmful.

Education without a system of values is hardly imaginable. The educational system of a particular nation represents the temperament and spirit of the culture of that nation. Our present system of education hardly helps students to develop their innate human virtues and prepare both for the mundane life and the hereafter, rather it paves ground for social parasitism, economic stringency and moral and spiritual bankruptcy. Present system of education is craving for the value based education. Looking at the present day youth, one is constrained to believe that he is almost devoid of all the basic virtues which characterize man for whom the universe has been brought into being. There is need of really good teachers who have some unique qualities about them. Duty of a teacher is not only imparting of information, but he is also expected to act as social reformer, moralist, nationalist, national integrator. Thus, Qur'an is like a torch for him which would give him light so that he will be able to remove the darkness of the society by giving right conduct, basic virtues and building character of the students who are the pillars of the society. It is the personality of the teacher, his efficiency and superior human qualities that influence the intellectual and the spiritual growth of the child. He builds up children to fit in the general social frame.

In the present time our society is facing the problems of student unrest, student indiscipline, disputes and frustration in the families. Solutions of all these problems can be found in this Holy Book of Qur'an. Qur'an provides a complete way of life, a complete code of conduct. It fixes the parameters of all that is in life and the world – one's routine, one's character, one's dealings, one's conduct, one's career, one's social life and above all the life hereafter. It teaches how to behave, how to earn, how to spend and how to live gracefully. It guides us on the path of a successful life. It also imposes sanctions and binds us to be fully responsible towards people around, family and friends in particular and the whole society at large. It integrates man with God, awakens in him **a new moral consciousness and invites him to deal with all the problems of life**—individual and social, economic and political, national and international – in accord with his commitment to God. Education of Qur'an aims at changing life and producing a new man and a new society, both committed to God and to the welfare of mankind. The Qur'anic universals provide us with the surest and most perfect guidance in all matters like actions, manners, morals, values, patterns of behaviour of the people; in fact all the ways of life as well as the angle of vision from which they look at other people of the world. They suit all times and all peoples.

Human society must proceed along the lines of Qur'anic Justice, equity, fairplay and brotherhood on a universal level. The code of life that the Qur'an presents is the strongest and the most powerful of all other man made codes. No other law, no other legal system, no other commands and prohibitions and no other rules and regulations are as inflexible, yet progressive, as those given by, the Holy Qur'an. There is a Direct Dialogue on the moral values and code of conduct. There is no other religious book where we find direct dialogue. Education alone is the strongest and most powerful force for the realization of life's end. Education which falls short of the envisaged aim and standard and which cannot provide the essentialities is prone to sidetrack the humanity and ultimately cause the world wide corruption and ruin. As the Holy Qur'an addresses human beings and human beings include people of all levels of intelligence, therefore, it is everybody's Qur'an. It is thought provoking for the philosophic mind that wants to go deep and deeper into finer and more subtle meanings of life. At the same time it invites all men to give serious thought to its contents and appreciate its wisdom not merely by word of mouth but by sustained action.

4

Philosophical Aspects of Qur'an

Philosophy is considered as a guide to the good life of man because knowledge about the nature of things. Education is philosophy in action. All people think, speak, act and behave as they learn through various agencies of education. Education concerns the whole man and the whole man becomes whole only when all the aspects of his life material, moral, social, spiritual, in fact all are developed equally well. It is said that each teacher has an educational philosophy of his own. A good teacher in addition to being a philosopher is a friend and a guide also. He remains constantly in search of permanent values of life because, by virtue of his rank of holding the greatest responsibility on this earth, he is expected to rise above the low levels of caste, creed, colour, nationality and the like to the higher concept of universal brotherhood of mankind.

The word and message of Allāh is conveyed to human beings in their own language; so does the Holy Qur'an. It uses the same words which are current in common vocabulary, but it uses with a difference. For example, it uses the same words for God, Prophet, Worship and Prayer etc., as have been in currency through ages among all the peoples of the world, but it either gives new meanings to them, or enhances their purport, or modifies their sense and thus clarifies all obscurities. For Philosophy the Qur'anic word is **'Hikmat'**, commonly translated as wisdom. Its root-word means "the strap of the rein with which the jaws of a horse are tied up." This strap prevents the horse from becoming unruly or going astray. To fix the rights and obligations and thus to prevent someone from exceeding limits is '**HUKM**'. *Hikmat*, therefore, means to fix with justice and correct proportion the rights and obligations of men and to prevent them from transgressions. A '**Hakeem**' or philosopher will, therefore, be one who sets things right in due order and proportion, beautifully, authoritatively and with a firm belief in the correctness of his decisions. In Verses 2:25, 4:113 and 6:89 we are told that the great Educators sent by Allāh to humanity as His Holy Messengers were equipped with the following four things integrated into one discipline called Nabuwwat:—**1. Law (*Kitab*, or the book), 2. Wisdom (*Hikmat*), 3. Authority (*Hukm*)** and **4. Knowledge (*Ilm*).**

Its first discipline, Law or the Book is the most perfect, complete and progressive way of life that gives practical training to people in keeping things in right order and correct proportion. Wisdom brightens up the understanding of the essence of each law and provides man's free will with right guidance towards and appropriate behaviour. Authority is necessary to protect both Law and Wisdom form the onslaughts of rebellious forces of Evil that work within man himself and outside of him. Knowledge has to subdue Nature for the common benefit and advancement of human society. Thus, knowledge is for the right understanding of relationships and for maintaining right order and discipline and correct proportion in them, and this ultimately leads to wisdom. Knowledge that subordinates not itself to the Divine Laws of the highest wisdom is worse than useless. It has an innate tendency to swerve towards arrogance and pride, and consequently, to upset the peace and order, tranquility and freedom. This, in a nutshell is essence of the Qur'anic philosophy of Education. Its main purpose is not only to criticize existing conditions or to offer suggestions for improvement, but also check authoritatively all vagrancies of thought and behaviour and to see that imbalances do not appear anywhere in relationships. The Qur'anic universals provide us with the surest and most perfect guidance in all matters like actions, manners, morals, values, patterns of behaviour of the people; in fact all the ways of life as well as the angle of vision from which they look at other people of the world. They suit all times and all peoples.

4.1 Metaphysics of Qur'an

It is said that Reality has an absolute and necessary, not merely contingent, existence. If smoke is rising from somewhere, we conclude that there is fire underneath it. Smoke is thus the "**sign**" of fire. The denial of "sign" is, therefore, the denial of Reality. Similarly, if a law is perfect, unchangeable and universally true then the maker of that law is decidedly perfect, unchangeable and universally true. The creator can be known only through the knowledge of his creation. All the tangible objects of the Universe are the Signs of this Reality. So are the laws which govern these objects. The Holy Qur'an enjoins upon us to contemplate the beauty, goodness and truth of the "Signs" scattered so profusely everywhere in the universe to have some knowledge of the Absolute Reality.

Tawhid is a revolutionary concept and constitutes the essence of the teachings of Qur'an. It means that there is only One Supreme Lord of the Universe. He is Omnipotent, Omnipresent and the Sustainer of the world and of mankind. The stars scattered through the almost infinite space, the vast panorama of nature with its charm and beauty, the planned waxing and waning of the moon, the astonishing harmony of the seasons – all point towards one fact; there is a God, the Creator, and the Governor. We witness a superb, flawless plan in the universe – can it be without a Planner? Truly Allāh said: O, Mankind: worship your Lord, who created you and those before you, so that you may ward off evil. It is an important metaphysical concept and answers the riddles of the universe. It points to the supremacy of the law in the cosmos, the all pervading unity behind the manifest diversity. It presents a unified view of the world and offers the vision of an integrated universe. It is a mighty contrast to the piecemeal views of the scientists and the philosophers and unveils the truth before the human eye. After centuries of grouping in the dark, man is now coming to realize the truth of this concept and modern scientific thought is moving in this direction. But it is not merely a metaphysical concept. It is a dynamic belief and a revolutionary doctrine. It means that all men are the creatures of one God – they are all equal. Discrimination based on colour, class, race or territory is unfounded and illusory. It is a remnant of the days of ignorance which chained men down to servitude. Humanity is one single family of God and there can be no sanction for those barriers. Men are one – black or white, Aryan or non-Aryan, Westerner or Easterner. Islam gives a revolutionary concept of the unity of mankind. The Prophet came to unite humanity on the word of God and make the dead live again. This concept also defines the true position of man in the universe. It says that God is the Creator, the Sovereign, and that man His vicegerent on the earth. This exalts man to the noble and dignified position of being God's deputy on earth and endows his life with a lofty purpose; to fulfil the Will of God on earth. This will solve all the perplexing problems of human society and establish a new order wherein equity and justice and peace and prosperity will reign supreme.

The second basic postulate of Qur'an is to **believe in the Prophethood of Muhammad (SAW)** was the last Prophet. And to believe in a prophet means to believe in his message, to accept the Law which he gave and to follow the Code of Conduct which he taught. Every prophet of God, according to the Qur'an, strove to build man's relationship with God on the principle of God's sovereignty and the acknowledgement of the authority of the prophet as the source of divine guidance. It is a part of their mission to translate guidance into practice, in their own lives and in the society they try to reform. All the Prophets are representatives of God, but they are human beings and their lives are models for mankind. Prophet Muhammad (SAW) is the last Prophet and as such the final model for mankind. To believe in him means to accept his authority as representative of the Supreme Ruler and to follow his example in thought and behaviour.

The third postulate of Islam is belief in the hereafter. The world according to Islam is a place of trial and man is being judged in it. He will have to give account of all that he does herein. Life on the earth will, one day, come to an end, and after that a new world will be resurrected. It will be in this Life after death that man will be rewarded or punished for his deeds and misdeeds. Those who live in the present world a life of obedience to the Lord will enjoy eternal bliss in the hereafter and those who disobey His commands will have to garner the bitter fruits of their disobedience. Whosoever professes these beliefs is a Muslim. And all these concepts are epitomized in the *Kalima*:

"There is no God but** Allāh; **Muhammad is His Prophet."

4.1.1 Meanings of Worship and Prayer in Islam

For '**worship**' the Holy Qur'an uses the word '**Ibadat**'. To understand the full concept of this word, we will have to consider the meanings of its root '*Abd'*. It is the name of a fragrant grass which the camel grazes with a relish because it makes them strong, sturdy and robust. But it also makes them extremely thirsty. To quench their thirst, the camel has to run for long distances in hot and arid deserts in search of water. From the ides of first undergoing hardships and then getting benefits as a reward for those hardships '*Abd*' came to mean a 'slave' who worked for his master and got from him all that he needed. *Ibadat* is, therefore, something done with a relish, hence, it is a work of devotion, love, fervour and a sincerity of the heart, something that is certainly beneficial not only physically, but also spiritually, giving full satisfaction to the mind, something that entails a little bit of hardship also, though this hardship is beneficial to him who undergoes it.

As a very important practical training in a number of disciplines it gives expansion to the human personality, evolves it and strengthens it. **Fasting** for a month which includes abstention from all physical pleasures as well from the free outlet of one's baser desires is a practical exercise in self control. **Pilgrimage** to the symbolic representation of humanity's centre of unity, where people gather from all parts of the world, strengthens the ties of brotherhood, expands relationships and creates an atmosphere of mutual love and understanding in addition to many other benefits. As all forms of Muslim worship are collective rather than individual, therefore, the prayers offered in mosques five times a day have special significance and meanings for the faithful. This '*Ibadat*', like all the other forms, trains him for full submission to Allāh's command, and unquestioning obedience to His Supreme Will.

A Muslim has to **pray five times a day**, before sunrise, between mid-day and afternoon, in the afternoon, immediately after sunset and between the time when the twilight is over and just before dawn. It means he cannot be forgetful of his dependence of Allāh and derives sustenance and new initiatives and strength this remembrance. Prayer prevents commits of Evil. *Salat* (prayer) is a compulsory form of worship, which is like an exercise towards which man is attracted with interest and willingness. He offers it continually, so, that his life may be free from all diseases and the body may be healthy and strong. The holy Qur'an and the *Sunnah* of the Prophet both are the open proofs of these realities. To keep away from evil, wickedness and to purify from bad deeds are also realities of the prayer.

These **prayers provide the most effective training in democracy**. Equality before Allāh five times a day is reflected as equality among men for the rest of the time also. The rich and the poor, the high and the low, the powerful and the week, the young and the old all stand shoulder to shoulder and all humble themselves equally together before Allāh. Coordination of efforts is yet another advantageous aspect of these prayers. All movements are performed in unison; the whole congregation raises together, bows on the knees together and prostrates to gather in perfect obedience of the command of the leader. When many people pray together in unison, spiritual emotion and fervour are heightened. A person offering his prayers dutifully at different hours spread over the day and a part of the night, remains always necessarily clean in body and dress. Washing the usually exposed parts of the body keeps one fresh all the day long. All Muslims inhabiting the globe turn their faces towards one symbolic centre of unity and fraternity. This strengthens the belief in the unity of Allāh, the unity of mankind and the unity of faith in a universal nationality.

Prayer is not in itself an end; it is rather **a means to achieve spiritual uplift of the individual as well as the society**. It undoubtedly improves a person's social morality and disciplines him to work persistently for mutual uplift in a democratic way. For individual and congregational prayers, not temples or churches are strictly necessary. Wherever an individual or group of individuals finds itself at the time of prayer, there and then prayer can be offered. A nation which has this conception of prayer and worship needs no special clubs, assemblies or even formalities. Prayer becomes an enlightenment and discipline for a pure and simple life and a mainstay of individual and social morality. Thus, Islam is the religion of life, it is not a belief in transcendental mysteries, dogmas or superstitions. It is a way of life determined by well organized philosophy of life and education which teaches all men that life is worth living and which gives a practical training for it.

4.2 Epistemological Beliefs and Postulates of Qur'an

4.2.1 Nature of Truth

The Qur'an uses the word '*Haque*' to signify Truth. This word is opposite in meaning to the word *Batil* (falsehood) and is concerned with faith (*Iman*) as well as practice (*Amal*). The Qur'an presents Islam as a way of life. This way of life is very comprehensive and it always takes a particular stand in every matter related to every aspect of life-personal, social or religious. Undoubtedly man is free to adopt any way of life. His freedom of choice and action is not restricted to the following any particular system of thought and practice. The Qur'an also accepts this fact (Anam, 107). But it invites human beings to adopt the Islamic way of life; it also discloses one more fact that the heavens and the earth and everything that exists between them are based on Truth, i.e. on Islam. As evidence to this claim the Qur'an invites us to study very minutely the creations of Allāh and to find out any flaw or defect in them. Or course man is unable to point out any flaw or defect in the creation of Allāh. The Qur'an says that these are based on Truth and are functioning on these principles free from any flaw and weakness. These bear witness to the fact that any thing which is not based on Truth can hardly work properly and live long. This indicates that man should not build the system of his life independent of God. We find quite clear ordinances in the Qur'an that Allāh has sent the Guidance and the Truth through His Prophets. In the light of these injunctions of the Qur'an it appears that whenever man, in any period of history, evolved any system of life independently he will certainly fail in his endeavour. To sum up, Islam consists of *Iman* (faith) and *Amal* (practice). *Amal* is related to the various aspects of life, i.e. social, economic and political. Islam, being a complete system of thought and practice appears in its sources as thought and practice appears in its sources as truth unchangeable and eternal. This has been called *Haque* (truth) and what is contrary to it has been called *Batil* (falsehood). And *Batil* like scum has no permanency.

4.2.2 Nature of Knowledge

> *"Read: In the name of thy Lord who created man from a clot. Read and thy Lord is the most Bounteous, who taught by the pen Taught man that which he knew not."*

These are the first verses revealed to the Prophet. The fact that the very first Qur'anic revelation is such a forceful exhortation for the acquisition of knowledge and that **knowledge is regarded as one of the great bounties of** Allāh **on human race**, is very significant and shows how closely Islam and knowledge identify with each other. It is indicative of the extreme importance that the new religion was going to attach to learning and knowledge. At the very outset it pronounces in the most unambiguous and unequivocal term its attitude towards knowledge and its dissemination which the new community was to take up as a sacred duty. Besides the open exhortations for the acquisition of knowledge, there are great many verses in the Qur'an which invite human beings to use their sense and exercise their reasoning faculties and thereby reach the ultimate truth. Moreover, Qur'an constantly encourages observation of the natural phenomenon at various places it stresses the necessity of the study of nature, the moon, the tide, the approaching night, the glittering stars, the dawning day, plants and animal life – all these have been presented in testimony of the law of nature and the power of the Creator. This is calculated to create a balanced and logical attitude which is so essential for the healthy growth of intellectual activity.

The Qur'an says that there is no limit to knowledge that the whole universe is made for and is subservient to man and that it is through acquisition of knowledge and use of reason that it can be conquered and made to serve the interests of mankind. The attitude of the Qur'an to knowledge and its acquisition is very positive and emphatic. Time and again it declares that acquisition of knowledge from any source and at any cost is the ordained duty of the believer. Qur'an assigns third place – only next to God and His angels – to those who possess knowledge, and rightly so. For, unless one has sound knowledge he cannot understand and appreciate the wisdom (*Hikmat*) of Qur'an, nor can he follow the tenets of the religion in its true spirit. Without knowledge one can neither know the commands of Allāh not be able to call others to the Eternal Truth. *Hadith* literature also confirms the same attitude towards knowledge. As in the Qur'an, learning has been praised lavishly in *Hadith* also. Learned people are declared and hailed as the best in the human lot and are designated as the successors and inheritors of the Prophets.

Islam presented a system of life built around a body of beliefs and a well defined approach to Man and society. The Islamic social order, built as it was on certain sound principles and practices unknown earlier to mankind, stood up as a unique innovation and experiment in human history. For proper running of the system, it was necessary that different components of the society were fully aware of their duties and obligations. The onerous responsibility of making the Muslims aware of their duties and educating them about their obligations was shouldered by the Prophet himself. At the same time it was also the enjoined duty of every member of the community to teach the fellow Muslims anything that he happened to learn from the Prophet or from any other Muslim. In this way knowledge was arranged to percolate down.

There is no intercession in Islam and the relationship between Allāh and man is direct. That is why Islam, more than any other religion, emphasizes the need to acquire knowledge. Quest for knowledge has always been an ideal in the history of Islam. Muslims of the early Islamic period undertook long and arduous journeys in search of knowledge. The prophet is reported to have said that those traveling in search of knowledge are in the path of Allāh till they return to their home. But this knowledge is not acquired through mysterious means. To acquire this knowledge, the student has to go through the process of comprehension, retention and remembrance of the facts; there is no other way to get hold of it. The high rank which Islam accords to the learned is evident from a *Hadith* which is to the effect that Allāh is most generous; it is his generosity that Allāh is most generous; it is his generosity that we get real knowledge from the prophet who is the most generous after Him because he transmits the entire divine teachings revealed to him and after the Prophet, that man is most generous who acquires knowledge and spreads it. Every sincere effort for the acquisition of knowledge is therefore, highly appreciated in Islam. The Prophet is reported to have observed that a believer would never be satisfied with good teaching till he reaches Paradise (*Ibid.*, p. 55). In Islam thus, knowledge is not regarded as an end in itself, but rather as a means for something higher and more sublime. The learned man is greedy of knowledge while the worldly man is greedy of wealth, these two are also not alike in their behaviour; the learned man calls others to follow right guidance whereas the worldly man summons the people to follow error (*Ibid.*, p. 42).

To Islam the source and the end of all knowledge is Allāh who is all Knowing (*Al-Aleem*). This knowledge has been transmitted to mankind through His different successive Prophets, as true teachers and educators, and has finally reached culmination in the teachings of the last Prophet of Islam. Islam is, thus, credited with bringing to the world a concept of knowledge and system of education and character building the like of which the world had not seen before and has not surpassed since. It enjoins every Muslim to seek and impart knowledge, not for its own sake, but for better living in this world and a more blissful and eternal life in the world hereafter.

4.3 Axiology of Qur'an

The Holy Qur'an is the **final revelation of truth and a code of the most perfect laws for humanity**. On account of his conscious and free will man holds a position of distinction and superiority over many of Allāh's creation. His creation is subject to the same rules and regulations which govern all other objects of Nature. These laws are obeyed unquestioningly by even the tiniest of atoms and the biggest of the heavenly bodies. Man however is, the only creation endowed with free will and he is likely to disobey, transgress limits or rebel. To prevent him from arrogant behaviour, it is but necessary that he should be governed by laws much higher than those which operate in the lower creation. The Qur'an brings the essentials of all knowledge within the purview of unchangeable basic realities of life which are so very important for man's happiness, peace and prosperity on this earth. Its truths and universal truths; its values are permanent values and its guidance is ever fresh for all the peoples of the world. The Qur'an approaches human problems realistically and in a serious and dignified manner. It offers the very best of practical and final solutions to them. These solutions are final because no better solution is possible for human intellect to think of. **The Holy Qur'an is a call for action**, not merely a sermon for recitation or enjoyment. Its commands and prohibitions are to be obeyed with full submission and conviction of the mind. Its each principle is to be followed meticulously as a sure guideline for a happy, prosperous life, free from fear and grief. **The Holy Qur'an's Message is for the whole of humanity**.

Like the Holy Qur'an the educators, too, have a message to convey, knowledge to import, nation to build and Truth to defend. How perfectly well they can do this depends upon the importance they give to the application of the principles of epistemology. The Message of the Holy Qur'an is free from complexities or doubts or suspicions, and therefore, it stands quite distinct form all other guiding literature. It contains values of life which are permanent and, at the same time, progressive. Its every word rejects superstitions, irrational beliefs, conjectures and whimsical credulities. Its promises are not based on guesses or actions which are in conformity with some progressively constructive thoughts about life. These thoughts are self-evident truths, and as such have their stability within themselves. They are, therefore, eternally and universally valid, hence permanent. They do not disregard the exigencies of time, hence, they are progressive. As no wisdom lies outside the Holy Qur'an, therefore, it is not merely a book of knowledge, it is rather knowledge itself. The greatness of Holy Qur'an lies in the fact that it gives to the world a comprehensive, practicable and faultless system of life which is idealistic and, at the same time, evolutionary. It provides copiously for not only the individual's development to its full and best capacity, but it ensures the collective social values also to come into free play.

Human society must proceed along the lines of Qur'anic Justice, equity, fairplay and brotherhood on a universal level. Each action, collective or individual, is to be weighed and measured against the standard values of the Qur'an. The code of life that the Qur'an presents is the strongest and the most powerful of all other man made codes. No other law, no other legal system, no other commands and prohibitions and no other rules and regulations are as inflexible, yet progressive, as those given by, the Holy Qur'an. It provides a powerful system of checks and balances through self-correction and mutual friendly admonition. In fact, the Holy Book is a living miracle. As the Holy Qur'an addresses human beings and human beings include people of all levels of intelligence, therefore, it is everybody's Qur'an. It is thought provoking for the philosophic mind that wants to go deep and deeper into finer and more subtle meanings of life. At the same time it invites all men to give serious thought to its contents and appreciate its wisdom not merely by word of mouth but by sustained action.

4.3.1 Some Moral Values of the Holy Qur'an

From the educational point of view, all social behaviour must emanate from the permanent values of life given by the Holy Qur'an; because Education itself is a continuous process in which the present generation of human beings passes on to its next future generation not only skills and attitudes, but also values beyond material goods. Thus, the permanent values of life form the nucleus of the Qur'anic Educational philosophy round which all educational activities must revolve, right from the elementary to the final stage of schooling. They must from the very moment it begins to suck its mother's breast. This is the only way to ensure world peace and security as changing values can never be trustworthy for even the simplest of men.

Tauhid ur rabubiyah: This permanent value is, in fact, the actualization of man's latent potentialities; hence, it forms the very base of the whole of our educational structure.

Bearing Duties and Responsibilities: To be responsible means to bear one's own burden, to accept open heartedly the consequences of exercising free-will. He must, at the same time, feely morally responsible to accept his weaknesses and failures.

Fulfillment of Promises and Agreement: Carrying out covenants is another permanent value of the Holy Qur'an. A covenant is to be looked upon as a solemn undertaking.

Justice: In a society in which justice is not practiced in daily affairs nothing remains in its proper place. Justice is therefore, the highest quality for which a Muslim has to stand firm as a witness of Allāh, even if it be against one's personal interests or against the interests of his dear and near ones.

Dispensation of Wealth: This is the basic principles on which stands the most unshakable structure of the economic system of the Muslims. Giving away goods to the needy is establishing truth in the eyes of the Holy Qur'an and, therefore, it is a permanent value.

Regard for Mankind: Men and women, children and adults are to be honoured not for any of their individual achievements, but on basis of equality simply because all are the descendants of the same ancestor.

Unification of Humanity: The Message of Allāh has always been for maintaining the unity of mankind. Differences spring up between individuals and nations through selfishness and egotism.

Knowledge and Understanding: Acquisition of wisdom and knowledge are permanent values to be endeared by all human beings.

Individual Effort: **"First deserve, then desire"**, is the well-known saying that gives, in a nutshell, the whole of the philosophy of the toil and struggle of life. To achieve a goal, one has to strive constantly, persistently and with perseverance.

Patience, Tolerance and Freedom of Choice: Man is free to chose between right and wrong as he wishes. Islam recognizes this freedom to the extent of a permanent value.

Purity/Celebacy: Spotless purity in thought, word and deed concerning one's self and concerning others is also a permanent value. The Holy Qur'an commands sex purity for both men and women, at all times.

Proper Usage of Wealth: According to Qur'an Wealth should be fully utilized. It should not be wasted.

Character-Building as the ultimate aim of the Qur'anic Education: There is a saying coming down from ages that if wealth is lost, nothing is lost; if health is lost something is lost; but if character is lost, everything is lost. The teacher is charged with the highest responsibility when he is asked to "train the will" of a humanbeing. Impulses and drives are the streams of man's energy. They rise somewhere in the unconscious, but come out into consciousness as pursuits and purposes. Hence, they rather form the very foundation on which character and personality are to be built. By their very nature they have a tendency to change, to clash with one another, to pass away or remain firm and develop, to take wrong direction or flow into directed channels, to grow into new habits, to take on new modes of thought, to follow ideas, to strive for objectives and to form a new type of personality or a social order. If they are suppressed, they are likely to cause maladjustments in individuals and in societies. They need, therefore, a proper guidance of reason from the earliest stage of childhood and even before the period when speech, conceptual thinking and self-consciousness begin to show up. This guidance is the beginning of character building. Character gets strength only when we are confronted with a situation in which we have to choose between higher and lower values we voluntarily sacrifice the lower value of "immediate gain" for a more solid and higher value of seeking the "Face of Allāh". Choosing the higher value is an act of "Faith" – yes, faith which carries forth every object of the Universe, step by step, to its self-fulfillment and self-realization.

According to the Holy Qur'an a **Believer, i.e. a Momin must have faith in 1. Allāh, 2. the Hereafter, 3.The unseen Celestial powers called Malaika (Angels), 4. The Book and 5. The Holy Prophets.** It must, however, be emphasized here that belief unaccomp0anied by action is no belief at all in the eye of the Holy Qur'an. From the educational point of view, these characteristics are to be considered not merely as desired traits of morality or the contents of a course of formal instruction in moral education or some important aspects of religious teaching, but as compulsory idealistic values which every child must possess and cherish. Anything falling short of these values is not acceptable to Islam, therefore, the educators cannot be permitted to select a few and leave out others according to their personal likings or disliking or the exigencies or times or social circumstance or political or environmental pressures.

Patience and **perseverance** bring firmness of character. Firmness is the sure road to success and prosperity. Enjoining right and forbidding wrong is yet another big responsibility that our young people have to shoulder. To bring ourselves up to the expectations of a really strong Ummah, we will have to consolidate all our assets, share our liabilities, pool our resources and readily take stock of our potentialities. Islam is not only a 'religion' of the Muslims, in the usual sense of the word; it is their whole life. It encompasses all aspects of human life: social, cultural, economic, educational, spiritual, material, political, in fact, all. A cult of universal brotherhood must, of necessity, be highly organized.

Enjoining right and forbidding wrong is yet another big responsibility that our young people have to shoulder. Belief in

Allāh, does not believe in His existence somewhere in the heavens far away from the human world. It is realizing His existence, His vitality, His Omnipotence, His whole Self, within every breath of ours, within every drop of blood that runs in the very essence of our being. It is submitting our whole spirit to the Supreme Will of Allāh, advancing His cause through our right behaviour and by leading a pure, chaste life, by working together in unison with Him. We have to follow His guidance at every step and work strenuously advancing His most beauteous, harmonious, perfect and proportionate scheme of universal evolution. This belief gets new strength, new vitality and new impetus the moment we examine our ideals, aspirations and activities critically. **Self-correction**, thus, provides us with checks and balances that are so necessary for smooth going in the world.

Maintaining right proportion in all affairs means not only a strong character, but a resolute and firm behaviour also. Justice can be done only when negation of all external pressure, influences and authorities etc., takes root within one's inner self and only Allāh's fear rules supreme. A deep knowledge of the Qur'anic injunctions regarding right and wrong behaviour and a clear notion of human rights, as given in the Holy Qur'an, is necessary for administering justice. Allāh commands us to do justice to all on equal footing, without the least possible hesitation, fear or favour.

If we have deviated from the right path inadvertently, we have to readjust our angle of vision and correct our direction even under pressures of adverse circumstances, or unfavourable conditions. If our gaze remains fixed on the ultimate objectives of our life, always and at all places, nothing in the world can overpower us or lead us astray. With this aim in view and by fixing our full attention on it, we can meet all situations daringly. So, let us adjust and readjust our direction as and when time demand.

5

Conclusion, Limitation and Suggestions

5.1 Conclusion

Education is the fundamental right of an individual, irrespective of the inherent social and personal differences, has not yet comprehended every human being. Universally, it is the privilege of every one to live in the world and learn. Learning and education is a necessity of life; and for living a complete and successful life education which is complete in itself is needed. It is this need of complete education which has caused the evolution of various educational systems from time to time; but none of them has gained the intrinsic value of being called ideal and perfect.

Education without a system of values is hardly imaginable. The educational system of a particular nation represents the temperament and spirit of the culture of that nation. Our present system of education hardly helps students to develop their innate human virtues and prepare both for the mundane life and the hereafter, rather it paves ground for social parasitism, economic stringency and moral and spiritual bankruptcy. Present system of education is craving for the value based education. Looking at the present day youth, one is constrained to believe that he is almost devoid of all the basic virtues which characterize man for whom the universe has been brought into being. The only thing that they consider is the market value of any field, or subject with better chances of admission to the university, regardless of whether the subjects opted by them for study are in conformity with their interests or not, whether they are in accordance with the demands of their society, that is absolutely of no concern to them. All this exhibits deterioration of our values, degeneration of ideals, and absence of any sense of responsibility. The human mind has become too materialistic and is making efforts to satisfy his ever increasing greed and passion. **The education which can aptly guide mankind to the true end is that which is envisaged in the Holy Qur'an—the unique of human guidance in all walks of life until the end of this world. The Qur'an deals with almost every aspect of the universe and reflects upon every basic problem of life until the end of this world. It is indeed the most comprehensive Book—the source of all information and inspiration—required to be followed by man to complete his mission of life by individual and collective endeavour.** The Qur'an has been believed, through misconception, as a scripture which dilates upon religious dogmas, folklores and rituals only. And on the basis of this misconception we have always been looking for light to the lanterns lit in the West, little realizing that we have our adequate resources, rich and resplendent, which if tapped and exploited properly and consummately, will unfailingly afford correct guidance not only to us but to the entire mankind.

The Holy Qur'an has come down from the Creator for the **guidance of mankind and which provides indicative light.** The Qur'an is like the rich and profound book of nature, with the difference that the Qur'an is articulate and eloquent while nature is silent. But its content and resources are equally inexhaustible, and will ever remain as fresh and novel. Every day it conveys a **new message to the humanity**. Allāh, the Exalted, revealed the Qur'an, to be a **beacon of light** that cannot be extinguished. It is a methodology and way of life that is perfect in all respects. In it is strength that cannot be equaled or repelled. It is the foundation of *Imaan* (Faith) and the spring of knowledge. It is the delight of the people of wisdom. The Qur'an is the greatest cure for all ailments. It is Allāh's Rope that cannot be severed. It is the Wise Reminder and the truly Straight Path. Allāh Almighty says that the Qur'an that the Qur'an was sent to Messenger Muhammad peace be upon him, to lead humanity out of darkness and into light.

The Qur'an is the unique book. **It is the fountainhead of all knowledge and wisdom, the source of divine inspiration, the best and most reliable code of human code of human conduct and the only guide to truth and salvation. It must be made the basis of all education and be made compulsory at all levels according to the requirements of age and comprehension. It should from the basis of the entire education, because it teaches discipline and obedience, and by virtue of it human character gets sanctified and the correct sense of value is developed.** Every man and women, young and old is enjoined to study the Qur'an which provides substance for thought and research, examples and similitude's for understanding and directions and guidance for acts of goodness and piety. They Qur'an has manifested the contrast between all that is positive and permissible and that which is negative and forbidden. In it have been specified all such things like, piety and sin, virtue and vice, truth and falsehood, right and wrong, faith and heresy, heaven and hell, love and hate, courage and fear, chivalry and cowardice, purity and profanity, obedience and intransigence, salvation and torment, forgiveness and revenge, honour and disgrace, justice and tyranny, knowledge and ignorance, charity and niggardliness, happiness and grief etc. Infact, there is not a single essential principle or aspect of life which is not expounded in the Holy Book. Education must therefore inculcate in children all such habits and features which are positively good and rewarding, and which discourage and prevent them from intentions and deeds which are illicit and harmful. Education alone is the strongest and most powerful force for the realization of life's end. Education which falls short of the envisaged aim and standard and which cannot provide the essentialities is prone to sidetrack the humanity and ultimately cause the world wide corruption and ruin. Today when we find that there are extensive fields of study, research and training and more mechanized means and facilities are available, the education all the same is not conductive to produce superior human qualities; rather it has miserably degraded man and offended the Maker of him. This agonizing situation has sprung up because our approach to education is unnatural, alien and absolutely antagonistic to our faith and ideology.

The next important religious subject is ***Hadith*** – the Traditions of the Holy Prophet, including the sciences of Islamic Theology and Jurispondence. The theories and principles, which the two sciences of Islamic Theology and Jurispondence deal with, concern an individual's personal development and self-purification, his obligations to and relations with his family, society and making, his occupation and livelihood, his day to day dealings in life and his association with the world around him. Such a subject of comprehensive and cyclopedia nature cannot be ignored. The two sciences must therefore find adequate representation in the educational schedule so as to make children intrinsically truthful, upright, cultured and progressively thoughtful.

The child in his early infancy is governed by certain laws of nature. He will develop properly if he is educated in the light of those laws. He has a natural tendency to accept what is pleasant, brilliant and attractive, and responds favourably to expressions of love and affection. He rejects what is unpalatable, ugly and obnoxious, and discards stern looks and anger. He needs education which conforms to his inherent attitudes and natural propensities. The child learns things more quickly and firmly in his tender age than in his later stages of growth and development. It is during his early years, after his birth or even before it, that an individual starts building his senses and forming his habits and sentiments. All those qualities which make man perfect and truly human may be acquired and developed at the initial stage and the rest of his characteristics which supplement the activities of his life could be acquired later with age and experience. So education, as a general principle, must first make man human and then professional.

As we know the success of education depends as much on the skillful teaching of the subjects as on the fitness of the curriculum. Much depends upon the teacher himself as the personality of the teacher, his efficiency and superior human qualities that influence the intellectual and the spiritual growth of the child. He builds up children to fit in the general social frame. **The Prophet of Islam was an educationalist and a teacher in the widest and truest sense of the world.** He was a teacher per-excellence. He remained a teacher all through his life. He taught the basic values, he taught his followers all that they needed for the betterment of this life and the life hereafter. And all this was achieved, not through preaching alone but also through the example of his own practice. Teaching is entirely unworthy if it is not put into practice. First of all a teacher should translate his teachings into practice. A teacher according to the Message of Qur'an should bear the role of a committed person. Teaching for him should not merely a profession of life. He should be committed to produce a virtuous generation of students. He should accept the greater responsibility of moral training than mere instruction to the subjects. A teacher is certainly the well wisher of his students. It is his prime duty to remove every shortcoming in them. He must play the role of a reformist in order to save his students from baseness and to inculcate in them goodness and piety. The teacher is the destiny-maker of the younger generation. Thus, it is the responsibility of the teacher to assess the intellectual and moral level of the students and to teach them accordingly, otherwise his efforts to educate the students will go in vain.

Man is not isolated in the accomplishment of his task of life. He has been made to live in a large society, with the assistance and cooperation of which he becomes able to maintain and develop his individual personality. In the world he has been assigned a specific part to play; his satisfactory performance depends upon the skillfulness, efficiency and integrity with which he seeks the support of his society and plays that part. He has **some social responsibilities** which he has to perform. Progress of a society depends considerably on its teachers and students. Selfless service to mankind irrespective of the considerations of caste, creed or kinship is the most glorifying deed of a true human being. **Charity or** *Zakat* has been made compulsory on the eligible 'scheduled' (*sahib Nisab*) persons. It awakens a sense of social responsibility in man, organizes human beings in a society and a state and enjoins the individual to subscribe to the social good. It also inculcates feelings of sympathy and love for the mankind in general and for the poor and afflicted in particular. A man's strength lies in his unity with his kinsfolk, friends and fellow men. Let the world adhere to the teachings of the Qur'an which are unquestionably genuine and beneficial, when all other instruction has failed in making the human race really literate and providing peace and happiness to the world.

5.2 Delimitation of the Study

Qur'an's guidance and Prophet's preaching's like a vast Ocean. It covers whole Universe, whole humanity, and complete way of life. So, study has been limited to only educational implications of Qur'an and *Hadith* and students, teachers and society are taken into consideration.

Present Dissertation is confined only to a brief study of Educational Implications of Qur'an and *Hadith* and it contains only those chapters of my Dissertation which are directly related to education. The Qur'an deals with almost every aspect of the universe and reflects upon every basic problem of life. It is indeed the most comprehensive Book – the source of all information and inspiration required to be followed by man to complete his mission of life by individual and collective manner. My dissertation is related to the educational implications of Qur'an. But it was impossible to concise whole ocean Qur'an guidance into a small dissertation like this. Its guidance and teachings are unending and unlimited.

I have taken only some permanent values of the Holy Qur'an and some selected Human Rights and Obligations and standards of a good character according to the Holy Qur'an and tried to find out their educational implications. All the values and all rights of Qur'an could not be enumerated and explained here. Therefore, my study is confined to explain only those universals which have a direct bearing on the educational philosophy. I have also discussed educational philosophy of the Holy Qur'an in brief in which I have taken Metaphysics, Epistemology and Axiology in short.

The Holy Qur'an's Message is for the whole of humanity; its teachings are meant for human beings; it addresses mankind. But it was impossible to take whole mankind into consideration. So, I took **teachers, students and society**. As teachers are the makers of the characters of the students and the builders of the society. So, I have tried to interpret that how the message of Qur'an could be helpful for the students, teachers and the society. Educational implications of *Hadith* are discussed wherever necessary. They could not be discussed in detail because in that case I would have to discuss the life history of Prophet Muhammad (SAW) and all the suggestions and teachings which he used to give to the followers as *Hadith* revolve round the Prophet. Do a brief introduction of *Hadith* is given and wherever needed its references are quoted. Main focus has been given to the Qur'an only.

As regards the five pillars of Islam and their educational implications; they have not been discussed separately. Five pillars of Islam have been mentioned and their brief introduction has been given separately. Their educational implications and benefits are there in the values of the Holy Qur'an and in the Philosophy of the Holy Qur'an.

5.3 Suggestions

There is wide scope of research in the area. The researcher suggests the following areas of search:

1. A comparative study of *Qur'an* and *Gita* can be done.
2. A comparative study of *Qur'an* and *Bible* can be done.
3. A comparative study of Islam and Jainism can be done.
4. The philosophical study of education of Islam in terms of Qur'an and *Hadith* can be done.
5. A study of Educational aspect during the period of the Prophet can be done.

6. A study of Relevancy of Islamic Education in the modern age can be done.
7. A study of the basis of educational theory in Islam can be done.
8. A critical study of the present Curriculum of Muslim Education can be done.
9. A study of the Educational system of Islam can be done.
10. A study of the philosophy of education of different Muslim philosophers and thinkers can be done.
11. A study of the causes of educational backwardness of Muslims in general and in India in particular can be done.
12. A study of psychological aspect of Qur'an can be done.
13. A study of the balance of knowledge and skills in Islamic education and culture can be done.
14. A study of Muslim education in India after Independence can be done.
15. A study of Astronomy in the Qur'an can be done.
16. A study of the Qur'an and Sex Education can be done.
17. A study of Qur'an and Social Responsibility can be done.
18. A study of Islamic economic order and its objectives can be done.
19. A study of women and Islamic Education can be done.
20. A study of Manners and Etiquettes in Islamic Education can be done.

5.4 Some Important Terms (Used Frequently in Islamic Literature)

1. **Bismillah** – In the name of Allāh.
2. **Din** – Way of life.
3. **Iman** – Faith and trust in Allāh (God).
4. **Momin** – A believer, a person who has deep faith in Allāh and is righteous and obedient servant of His.
5. **Kufr** – To show ungratefulness to God and not to believe in Him and His religion.
6. **Sajda** – Prostration (bowing to God), worship, adoration

7. **Wudhu** – A purification (ablution) that must be performed before someone does their *Salah* or reads the Qur'an.
8. **Shaitan (Satan)** – is the source of evil in the world. The plural name is *Shayatin*. He always tries to misguide and mislead people. The Qur'an states that Satan is not an angel but a member of the *Jin*. His other name is *Iblis*.
9. **SAW** – Abbreviation for *Sallallahu alaihi wassallam* meaning may blessing and peace of God upon him (Muhammad). It is said when the name of Prophet is mentioned.
10. **PBUH** – Abbreviation for the words – Peace be upon him or her. It is said when the name of Prophet is mentioned. It is generally used by the English speaking people.
11. **Malaik** – Originator of Creation. Also the Angels.

Bibliography

Agrawal, A. (1980). *A Study of the Impact of Education on Social and Cultural Modernisation of Hindu and Muslim Women*, Kumarkam University, Ph.D. Education, Indian Educational Abstract, New Delhi: NCERT.

Ahmed, Khurshid (1977). *Islam: Its Meaning and Message*, New Delhi: Ambica Publications, pp. 21-26, 315-16.

Ahmed, Manzoor (1990). *Islamic Education: Redefinition of Aims and Methodology*, New Delhi: Qazi Publishers and Distributors.

Ahmed, Naseem (2003). *Islamic Manners* (Vol. I), *Life and Society*, New Delhi, Anmol Publications Pvt. Ltd., pp. 3-38, 191-98, 269-82.

Ahmed, Naseem (2003). *Islamic Manners* (Vol. II), *Ideals of Life*, New Delhi: Anmol Publications Pvt. Ltd., pp. 3-86, 133-140.

Ahmed, S. Akbar (1992). *Post Modernism and Islam Predicament and Promise*, London and New York.

Ahmed, S. Akbar (1993). *From Samarkand to Stornway Living Islam*, London: BBC Books Ltd., Woodlands.

Ajetunmodi, Musa Ali (1985). *The Basis of Islamic Economic System, Islam and the Modern Age*, Vol. XVI, No. 4: 215-22.

Alam Zafar (2003), *Islam Education Theory and Practice*, New Delhi: Adam Publishers and Distributors, pp. 1-32, 54-62, 64-71, 87, 93-98.

Ali, Abdullah Yusuf (1934) (Reprint 1949). *The Message of Islam*, London: John Murray.

Ali, Asghar (1980). *The Origin and Development of Islam*, Bombay: Orient Longman.

Ali, Asghar (1983). *Islam and its Relevance to Our Age*, Bombay: Institute of Islamic Studies.

Ali, Asghar (1984). *Islam and Revolution*, Delhi: Ajanta Publications.

Ali, Asghar (1985). *The Status of Women in Islam*, Bombay: Institute of Islamic Studies.

Ali, K. (1986). *A Study of Islamic History*, Idarah-I-Adabiyat-I-Delhi, Qasimyan Street, Delhi.

Ali, Maulana Muhammad (1938). *Introduction to the Study of the Holy Qur'an*, Lahore: The Ahmadiya Anjuman Ishaat Islam.

Ali, Maulana Muhammad, *The Religion of Islam*, New Delhi: S. Chand & Company Ltd.

Ali, Syed Ahmed (1964), *Economic Foundations of Islam*, London: Orient Longmans.

Ali, Syed Amir (1978). *The Spirit of Islam*, Idarah-I-Adabiyat-I-Delhi, Qasimyan Street, Delhi.

Anderson, J.N. (1965). *The World Religions*, London: Frank Cass, pp. 315-16.

Ansari, A.A. (1988). *Educational Philosophy as Found in Islamic Culture*, University of Bombay, Fifth Buch Survey (Vol. II) (1988-92), NCERT.

Arberry, A.J. (1964). *Aspects of Islamic Civilization*, London: Frank Cass.

Arnold, Thomas and Guillaune R. (1968). *The Legacy of Islam*, Oxford: Oxford University Press.

Asad, Muhammad, 1934 (Second Edition 1969). *Islam at the Cross Roads*, Lahore: Arafat Publications.

Azad, Maulana Abul Kalam (1962). *The Tanjuman Al-Qur'an*, Vol. I (Surat-ul-Fatiha) Edited and Rendered into English by Dr. Syed Abdul Latif, Bombay, Asia Publishing; Bell, R., 1926, *The Origin of Islam in its Christian Environment*, London: MacMillan.

Bhave, Vinoba (1962). *The Essence of Quran*, Varanasi: Sarva Sewa Sangh Prakashan.

Calverley, E.E. (1958). *Islam: An Introduction*, Cairo: The American University.

Caselli, Aldo (1957). *An Interpretation of Islam*, Translated by Veccia veglieri, Lama Washington: American Fazi Mosque.

Cragg, Kenneth (1969). *The House of Islam*, Belmont, California, Dickenson Publishing Co.

DeBoar, T.J., *The History of Philosophy in Islam*, New York: Dover Pub. Inc.

Fakhry, Majid (1970). *A History of Islamic Philosophy*, New York: Columbia University Press.

Farias, (1981). *Religious Commitments of Muslim Students in Bangalore: A Study of Relationship between Religion and Social Situation*, AMU, Indian Educational Abstract, New Delhi: NCERT.

Faridi, Shahidullah (1985). *Inner Aspects of Faith*, Delhi: Noor Publishing House.

Firoz, Syed (1995). *A Study of Religiosity and Values*, Indian Educational Abstract (Issue 4, Jan 1997), New Delhi: NCERT.

Fyzee, Asaf A.A. (1963). *A Modern Approach to Islam*, Bombay: Asia Publishing House.

Gribbm, H.A.R., and Kramers, J.H. (1974). *Shorter Encyclopaedia of Islam*, Leiden: E.J. Brill.

Grunebaum Von, G.E. (1970). *Classical Islam a History* 600-1258, London: George Allen & Unwin Ltd.

Gupta, B.S. (1980). *Equality of Educational Opportunities and Muslims*, Bhopal University, Indian Educational Abstract, New Delhi: NCERT.

Hameed, Abdul Hakeem (1981). *Islam at a Glance*, New Delhi: Vikas Publishing House.

Hamidullah, Muhammad (1957). (Second ed. 1959) *Introduction to Islam*, Paris: Centre of Cultural Islamique.

Hanif, N. (1997). *Islam and Modernity*, New Delhi: Saroop & Sons.

Haq, Mahar Abdul (2002). *Educational Philosophy of the Holy Quran*, New Delhi: Adam Publishers and Distributors, pp. 1-15, 63-79, 240-273, 324-353.

Hartung, John Peter, Reifeld Helmut (2006). *Islamic Education, Diversity and National Identity*, New Delhi: Sage Publications, Thousand Oaks, London.

Hayaket, Muhammad Husain (1976). *The Life of Muhammad*, North American Trust Co.

Hitti, Philip K. (1970). *Islam a Way of Life*, London, Bombay, Karachi, University of Minnesota Press, Oxford University Press.

Hosain, Saiyed Safdar (1985). *The Early History of Islam*: Vol. 1, *Life of the Holy Prophet Mohammad*, New Delhi: Prabha Publications.

Hussain, S.M., Azizuddin (2005). *Madarsa Education in India, Eleventh to 21st Century*, New Delhi: Kanishka Publishers & Distributors.

Iqbal, Afzal (1986). *Dimensions of Islam*, Idarah-I-Adabiyat-I-Delhi, Qasimyan Street, Delhi.

Iqbal, Sir Mohammad (1934). *Reconstruction of Religious Thought in Islam*, Oxford University Press, London, First Indian Edition, 1980, Delhi: New Taj Office.

Iqbal, Sir Mohammad (1944). *The Secrets of The Self*, Trans., by R.A. Nicholson, Lahore, Ashraf, 1944, Original Persian title, *Asrar-i-Khudi*, 1915, Lahore.

Jameelah, Maryam (1983). *Islam in Theory and Practice*, Delhi: Taj Company.

Jeffery, A. (1958). *Islam, Mohammad and His Religion*, New York: Liberal Art Press.

Khalifa, Mohammad (1983). *The Sublime Quran and Orientalism*, New York: Longman.

Khan, Maulana Wahiduddin (1995). *Islam Creator of The Modern Age*, New Delhi: Idara Isha'at-e-Diniyat (P) Ltd., Hazrat Nizamuddin.

Khan, Muhammad Sharif (1996). *Education, Religion and Modern Age*, New Delhi: Ashish Publishing House, pp. 1-19, 21-35, 103-117.

Khan, Muhammad Sharif (1997). *Some Aspects of Islamic Education*, Ambala Cant, The Associated Publications, Haryana.

Khan, Muhammad, Zafrulla (1962). (2nd ed. 1980), *Islam : Its Meaning for Modern Man*, London: Routledge and Keagan Paul Ltd.

Lammens, H. (1929). (New Impression 1968) *Islam-Beliefs and Institutions*, Trans. By Sir E. Denison Ross, London: Franc Cas & Co. Ltd.

Latif, Sayyid Abdul, *The Concept of Society in Islam and Prayers in Islam*, Lahore: Muhammad Ashraf.

Leuris, B., Pellat, Ch., and Schacht, J., (1965). *The Encyclopaedia of Islam*, Leiden: E.J. Brill.

Levy, Reuhen (1957). *The Social Structure of Islam*, London: Cambridge University Press.

Lion Handbook (1982) (1st ed.) Rep. (1983). 84, 85, 88, *The World's Religions*, England: Lion Publishing Plc.

Maududi, Syyid Abdul Ala (1963). *Towards Understanding Islam*, Lahore, Islamic Publishers Ltd., Translated and edited by Khurshid Ahmed (Original Publication 1940), pp. 10-11, 17-19, 27-32.

Moazzam, Anwar (1981). *Islam and Contemporary Muslims World*, New Delhi: Light and Life Publishers.

Mondal, Sekh Rahim (1997). *Educational Status of Muslims*, New Delhi: Inter India Publications.

Nadwi, Abdul Hasan Ali (1959) (Second ed. 1967). *Islam and The World*, Lukhnow: Academy of Islamic Research Publications.

Nasr, Sayyed Hossain (1966). *Ideals and Realities of Islam*, London: George Allen & Unwin.

Nehvi and Lidhu (1966). *Educated Muslim Women in Kashmir: Their Attitude Towards Tradition Verses Modernity*, Indian Educational Abstract, Issue 2 (Jan, 1997), New Delhi: NCERT.

Noss, John Boyer (1949) (6th ed. 1980). *Man's Religions*, New York, MacMillan Publishing Co.

Padal, Mirza Abdul (1924). *Sayings of The Prophet Muhammad*, Allahabad: Reform Society.

Pandey, J.B. (1985). *A Comparative Study of Educutional Philosophy in Gita and Qur'an*, Kumarkam University.

Pickthall, Muhammad Marmadukee (1927). *Cultural Side of Islam*, Lahore: Sheikh Muhammad Ashraf.

Pickthall, Muhammad Marmadukee (1977). *The Glorious Qur'an, Text and Explanatory Translation*, Rabita Mecca, Muslim World League.

Qasmi, Muhammad Sajid (2005). *Madrasa Education Framework*, Mumbai (West), Markazul Ma'arif Education and Research Centre (MMERC), Jogeshwari.

Qazi, Naseem (1985). *The Concept of Man in Islam*, Rajasthan University, Jaipur, Rajasthan.

Qureshi (1960). *Study on Muslim Education and Learning in Gujarat* (1297-1758).

Qutb Muhammad (1968). *Islam, the Misunderstood Religion*, Delhi: The Board of Islamic Publications (First Indian edition).

Rahman, S.H. (2005). *Education under Islam*, New Delhi: Ref. Press.

Rahman, Zikr-ur (2004). *Islamic Principles*, New Delhi: Anmol Pub. Pvt. Ltd., Ansari Road, Daryaganj.

Rajwade, *Status of Muslim Women in Indore City: A Case Study*, Indore University (PhD Sociology). Madhya Pradesh.

Rashid, Khwaja Abdul (1960). *Essays of Islam*, Karachi: Din Muhammad Press.

Rehman, Fazlur (1996). *Islam*, Weindenfeld and Nicolson, London.

Rizvi (1986). *Study on Curriculum: Aim of Muslim Education.*

Sell, Edward (1880). Reprint (1982). *The Faith of Islam*, Muslim Academy Press.

Seshagiri Rao. K.L. (1969). *Islam, Guru Nanak Quincentenary Celebration Series*, Patiala: Punjabi University, Punjab.

Shalabi (1954). *Study on the Curriculum of Muslim Education.*

Sheikh, Wahid Baksh (2003). *Education Based on the Teachings of Holy Qur'an*, Delhi: Adam Publishers & Distributors, pp. 15-18, 31-37, 81-95, 97-125.

Sheikh, Youssef-ul-Digwy (1982). *Islam the Ideal Religion*, Trans by Aly, Z., Hushy, Delhi: Taj Company.

Siddiqui, Prof. A.H. (1982) (1st Ed.), 1985 (2nd Ed.). *Life of Muhammad*, Delhi: Hindustan Publications, Qasimjan Street.

Smith, W.C. (1957). *Islam in Modern History*, New Jersey, Princeton University Press.

Sufi (1941). *Study of the Evolution of Curriculum in the Muslim Educational Institutions of India.*

Tames, Richard, (1982). *Approaches to Islam*, London: John Murray.

Thanvi, Maulana Ashraf Ali (1985). *Hayaatul Muslimeen*, New Delhi: Adams Publishers.

UNESCO, (1980) (June), *Islam, Philosophy and Science*, four public lectures organized by UNESCO, UNESCO Press.

Waddy, Chris, (1976). *The Muslim Mind*, London: Longman.

Waliullah, Shah, (1941). *Islamic Philosophy.*

Watt, W., Montgomery (1968) (Second Ed. 1979), *What is Islam?* London: Longman.

Welch, T. Alford, and Cachia Pierre (1979). *Islam Past Influence and Present Challenge*, Edinburge University Press.

Wojtilla, Gyula (1983). *Contribution of Islam to World Civilization and Culture*, New Delhi, Jammu, Trivandram: Light and Life Publications.

Zia Ullah, Mohammad (1984). *Islamic Concept of God*, London: Kegan Paul International.

Internet Websites

1. Islam Online.net
2. Islam.com
3. www.DivineIslam.com – (Qur'an Viewer Version 2.910)
4. www.islamasoft.co.uk
5. www.yildun.com
6. www.harunyahya.com
7. muslimunited.org
8. www.alrisala.org
9. The Hadith Software

صَدَقَ اللّٰهُ الْعَلِيُّ الْعَظِيْمُ

Index